the interior designer's
drapery
sketchfile

the interior designer's
drapery sketchfile

edited by Marjorie Borradaile Helsel, A.I.D.

Whitney Library of Design

Copyright © 1969 by Marjorie Borradaile Helsel

First published 1969 in New York by Whitney Library of Design,
an imprint of Watson-Guptill Publications,
a division of Billboard Publications, Inc.,
1515 Broadway, New York, N.Y. 10036

Library of Congress Catalog Card Number: 68-58182
ISBN 0-8230-7289-4

Manufactured in U.S.A.

First Printing, 1969
Second Printing, 1974
Third Printing, 1975
Fourth Printing, 1977

contents

preface

This, the first in a series of sketchfiles now under way, is a reference work that I hope will be as welcome on your desk as it is on mine. In fact, my principal motivation in assembling this comprehensive collection of drapery designs in one efficient volume is the almost daily need for this design tool in my own office.

In actual use, I visualize the drapery sketchfile filling three distinct roles. First, as a design tool. Second, as an idea source. Third, as a catalog.

Many of its sketches may be traced *per se* to supplement workroom orders and instruct workroom personnel. Therefore, in its role as a design tool, the sketchfile can provide the actual drawings from which custom-made draperies and valances may be produced. Hopefully it will fill the vacuum of available illustrative material in this area of homefurnishings, short of the designer making new sketches on each occasion.

Others of its designs may be quickly adapted to fit the requirements of a current job or an immediate problem. Or just thumbing through the sketchfile may trigger an idea that leads to a fresh and original creation. As an idea source, this reference work should expand the professional designer's library in an area that is barren at present.

It is easily conceivable that *the interior designer's sketchfile* might also prove a much-needed catalog of the custom-furnishings field. Within the following pages, for example, is an impressive selection of drapery and valance designs for a client to "see" without the designer having first to invest precious drafting time or accumulate costly samples. Freed from this speculative or preliminary phase, the designer may put his time to more productive work.

I have observed that the efficiency of a reference volume is directly related to how retrievable its information really is. But this specific subject matter, drapery designs, seems to permit only the broadest indexing and still retain the spontaneity that will make it idea-sparking. Therefore, only basic categories have been established: the obvious **period designs,** which logically correspond to the traditional breakdown of furniture styles; **formal designs,** which can easily overlap the previous category; the remaining conglomerate, **casual designs;** the very brief **headings** which illustrate the various types of pleating; tie-backs, concentrating more on the variety of materials employable to hold back draperies rather than methods (for, after all, there are only a handful of ways to physically tie a drapery back) and finally, **valances,** the change of which can create a completely new drapery design.

While it is presumptive to think that any treatment of this subject might be exhaustive, every attempt has been made to cover its logical sub-divisions. Sizes and types of windows have been considered. Styles of interiors and the ages and sexes of occupants have been taken into account. Since the designer himself will know whether a drapery design will scale up for a hotel lobby window or belongs in a man's private study, explanatory copy has been omitted almost entirely. Drawings are annotated only where it seems desirable to supplement the meaning or suggest a certain material. Otherwise it is hoped that the sketches will speak for themselves.

All in all there are some 292 different sketches included in this work. Lest it become too voluminous to be practical, valance and tie-back ideas once illustrated in the earlier period, formal and casual design sections; are not repeated in the specific sections for these two topics. Purposely omitted, too, are blinds and shades, which supplement or sometimes supplant drapery treatments. They will follow in a separate sketchfile.

Marjorie Borradaile Helsel, A.I.D.

period designs

Renaissance

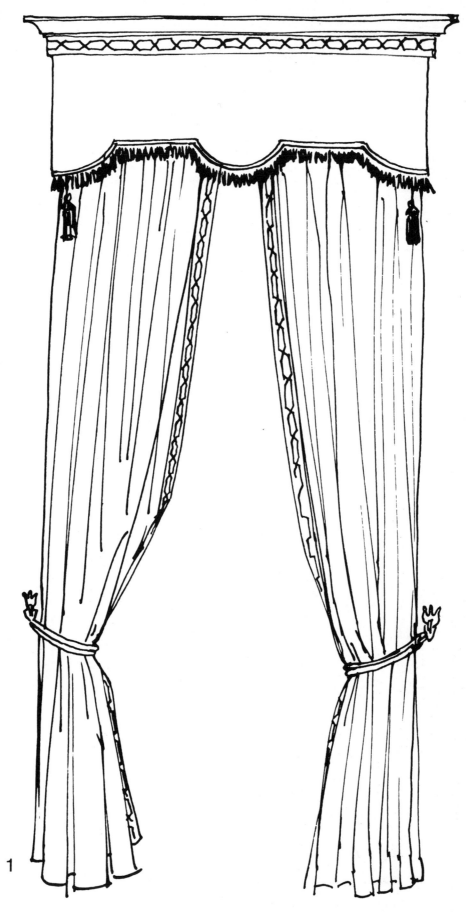

1

Renaissance

flat fabric panels
with
embroidery

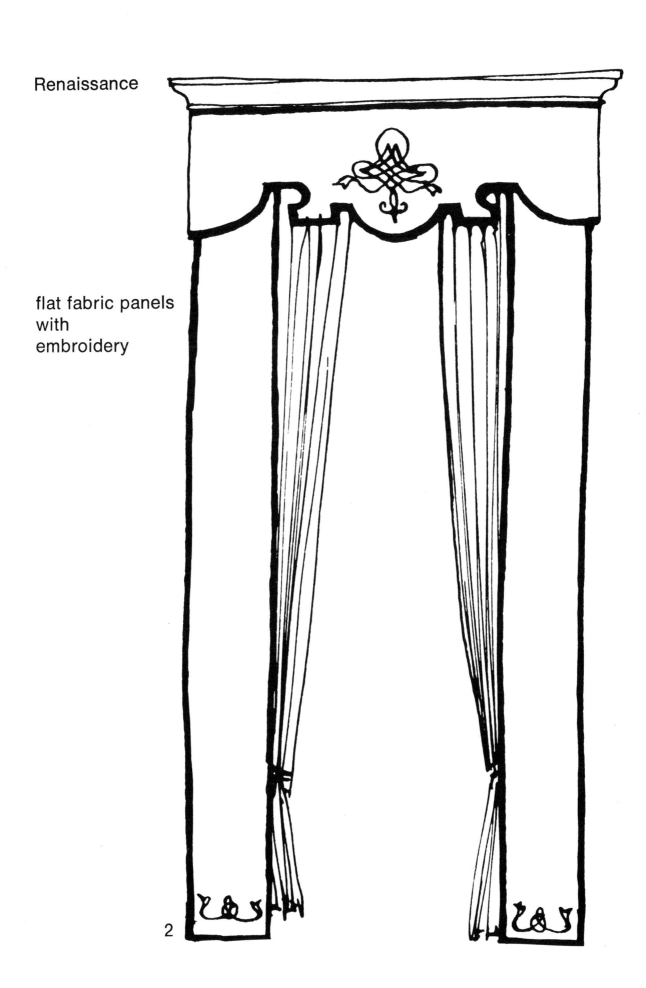

2

Renaissance

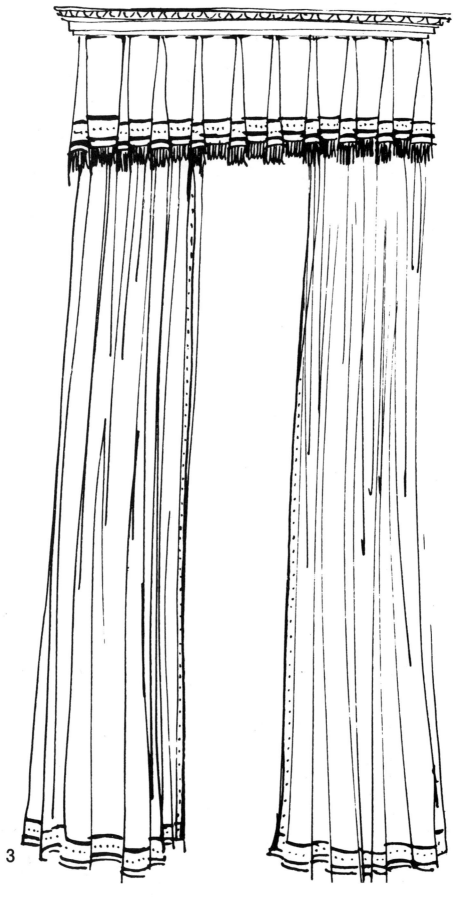

3

Renaissance

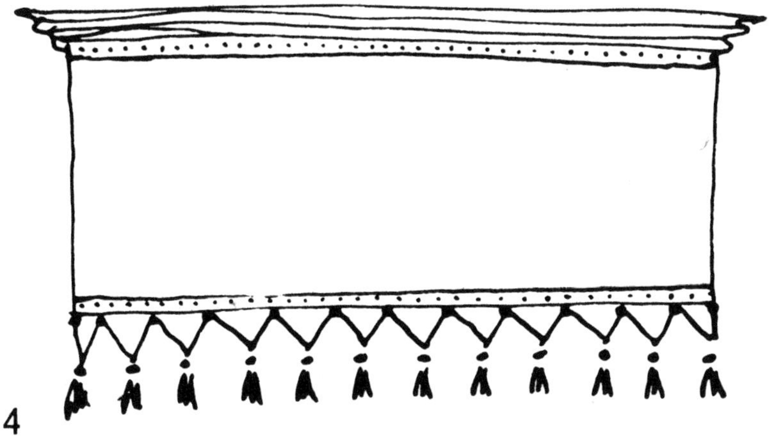

4

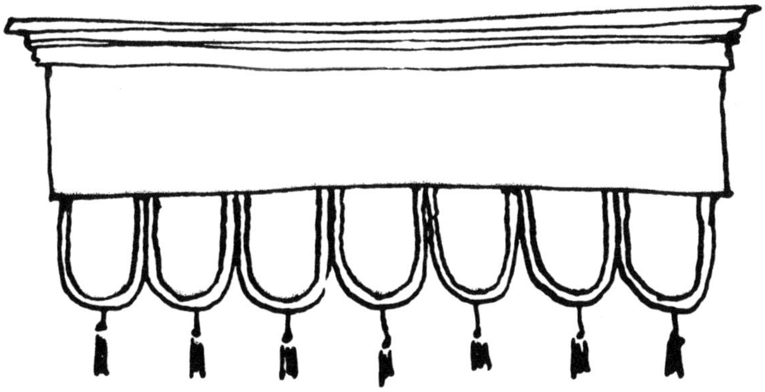

5

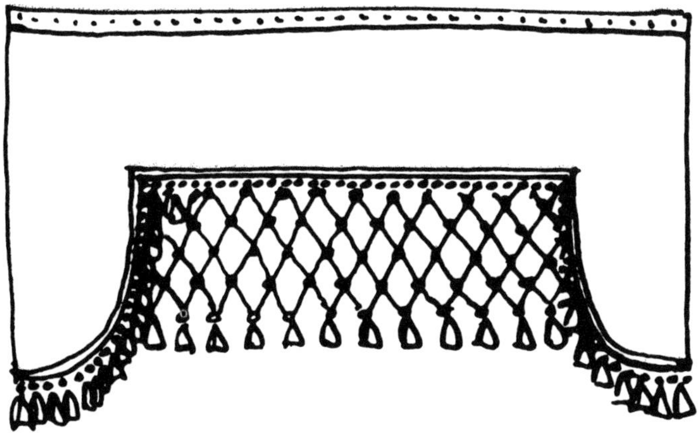

6

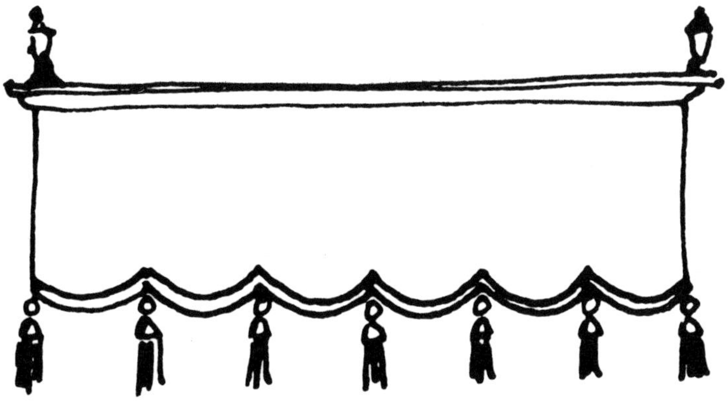

7

Louis XIII

flame stitch

8

Louis XIII

9

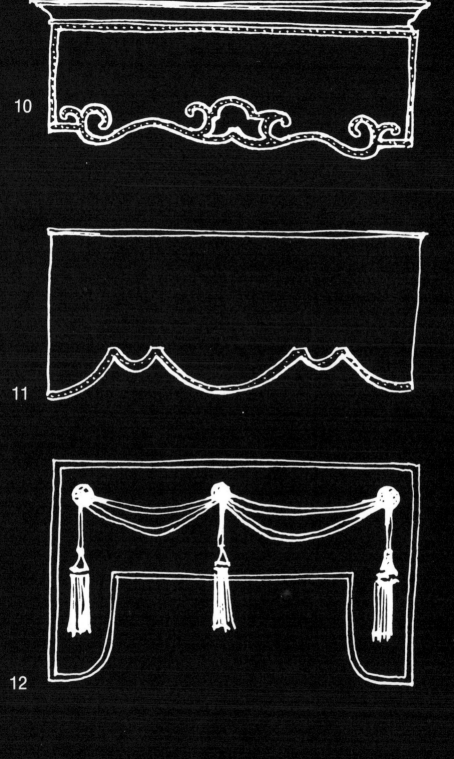

Louis XIV   Louis XIV

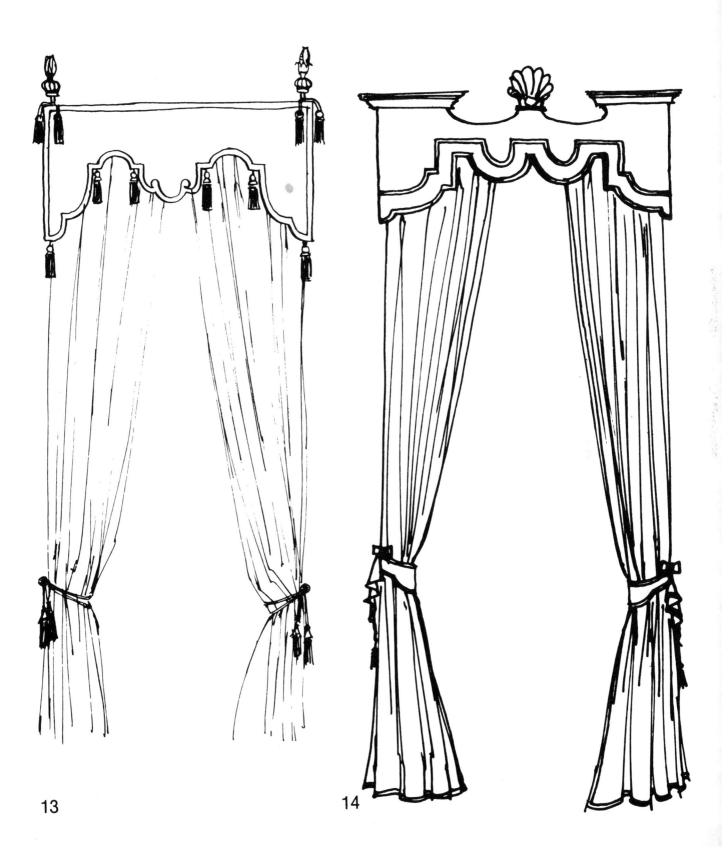

13   14

Régence

Régence

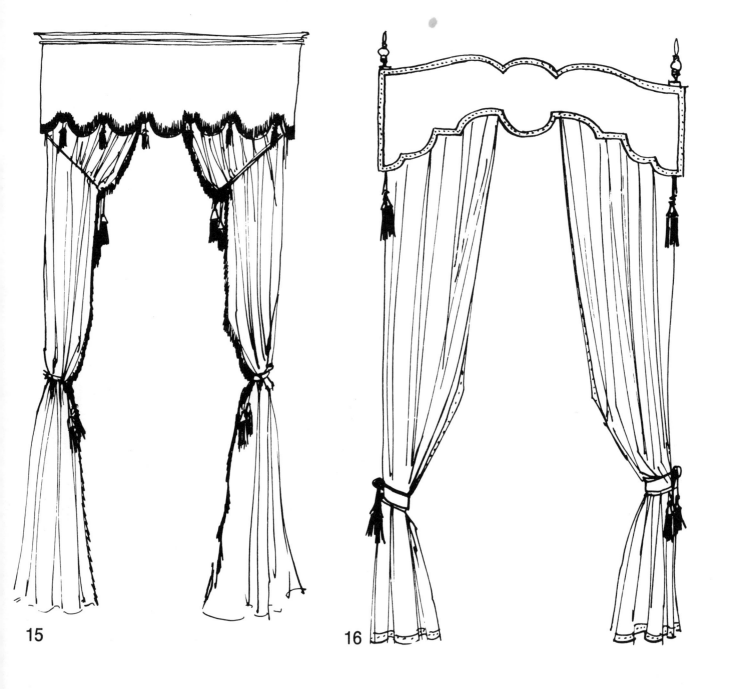

15

16

Louis XV

Louis XV

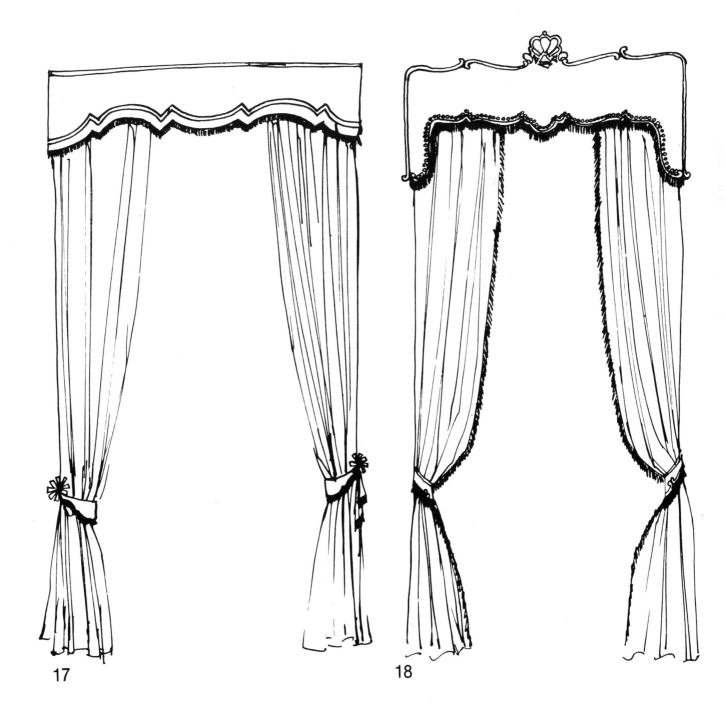

17

18

Louis XV

19

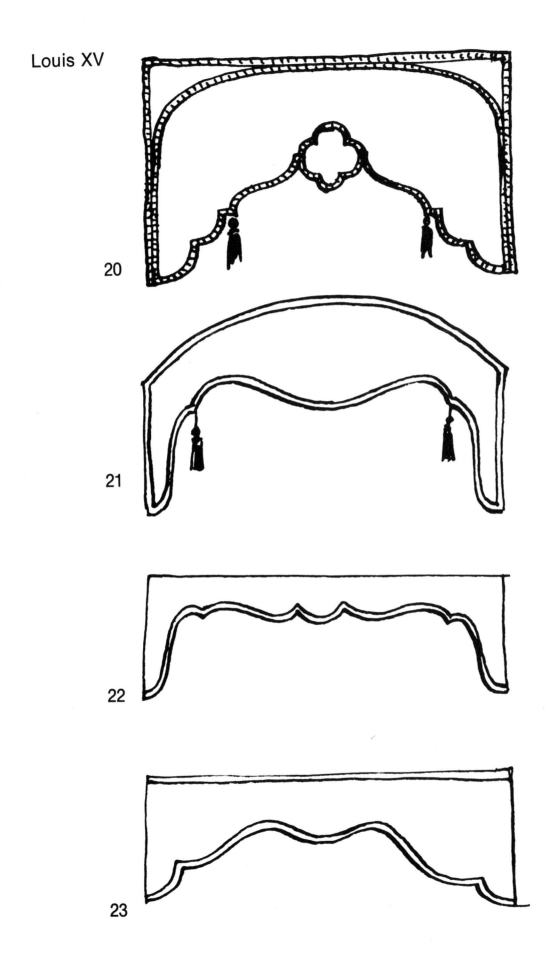

Louis XV

20

21

22

23

Louis XVI

24

Louis XVI

25

Louis XVI

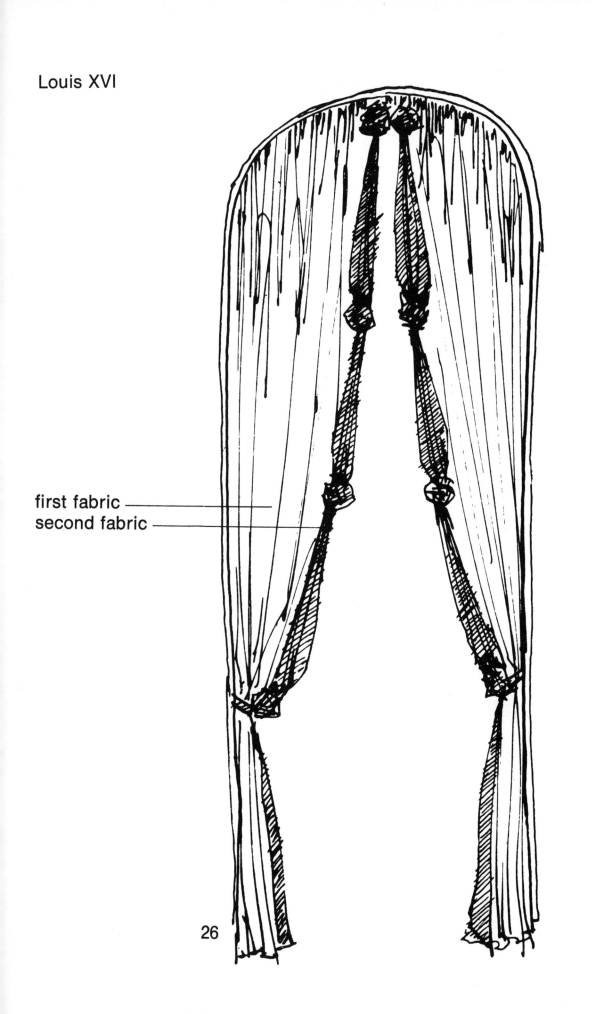

first fabric
second fabric

Louis XVI

27

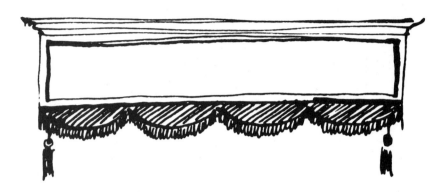

28

29

30

31

Louis XVI

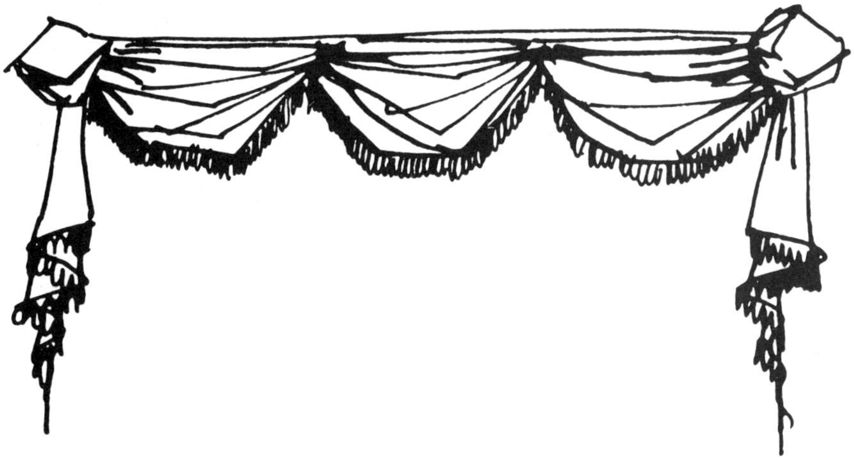

32

fabric rosette

33

34

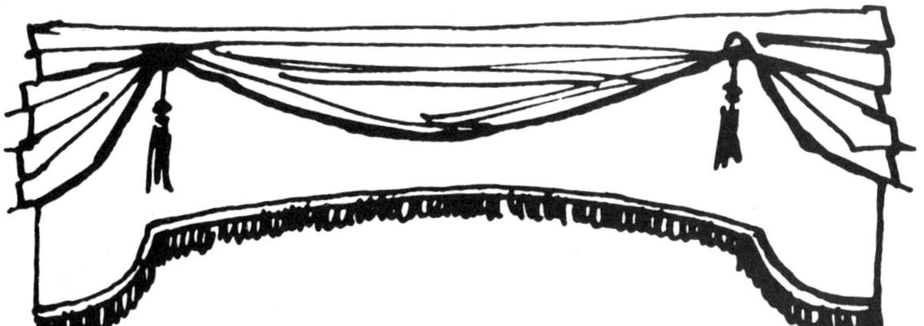

35

36

37

Directoire

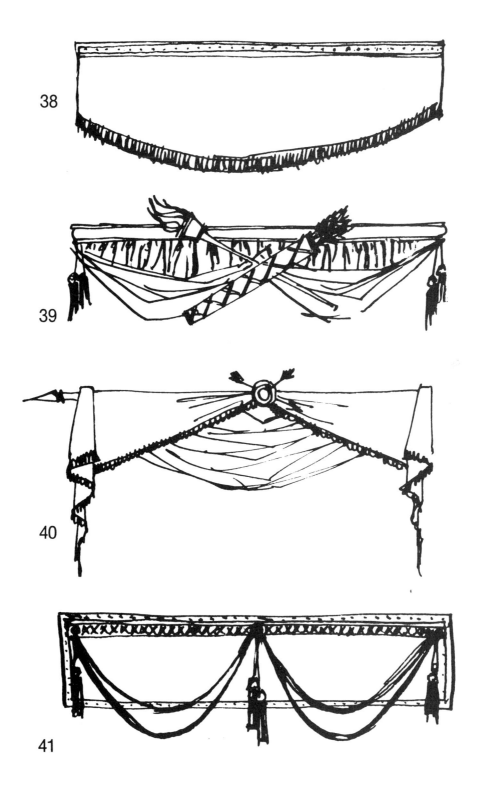

38

39

40

41

Empire

42

Empire

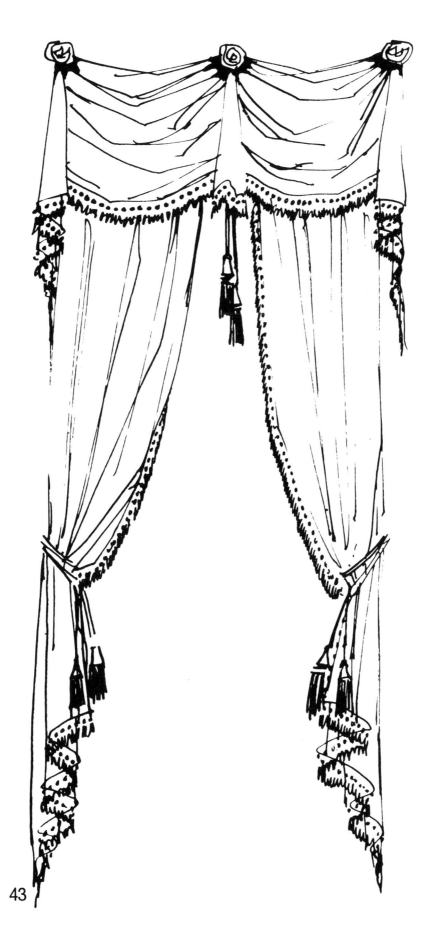

Empire

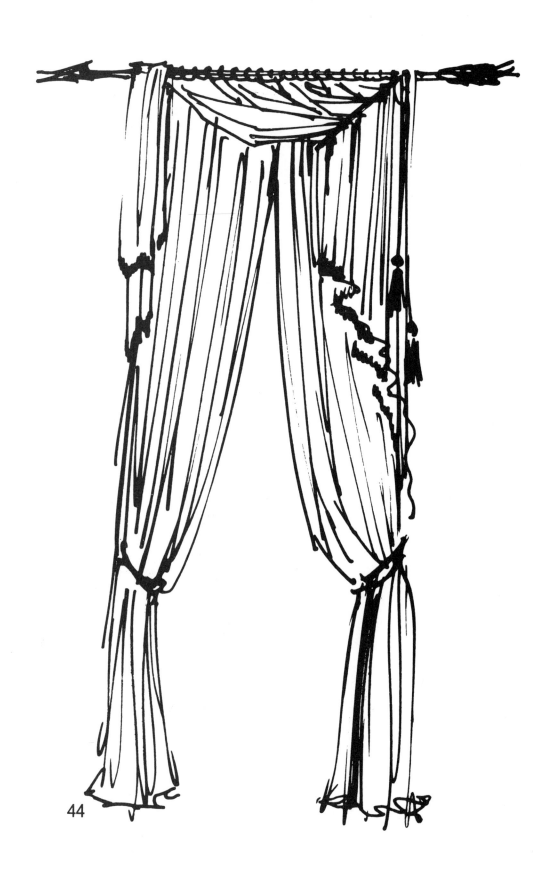

44

Empire

45

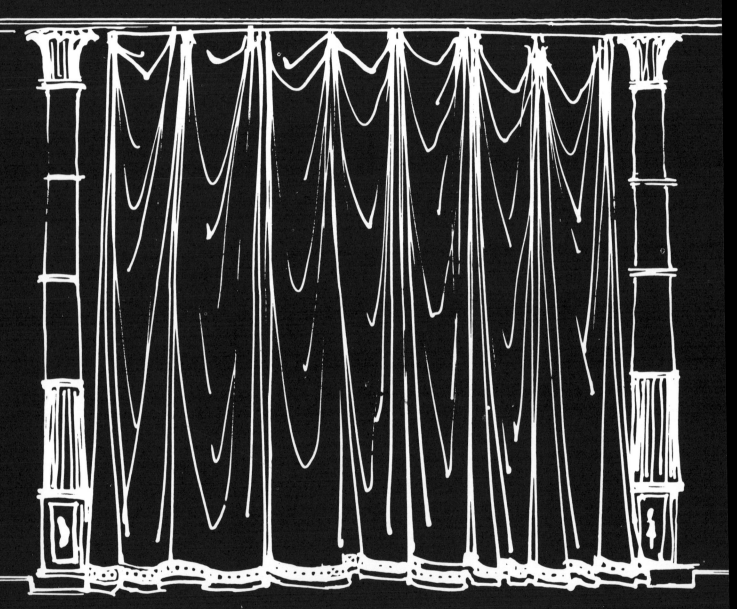

46

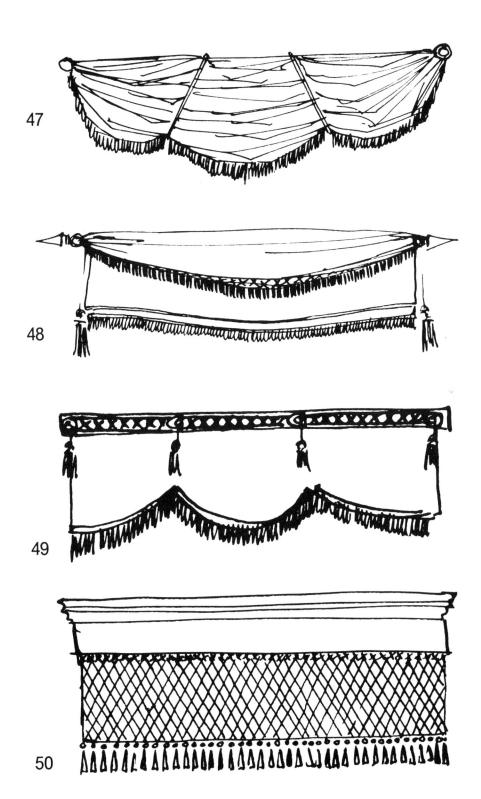

47

48

49

50

Queen Anne

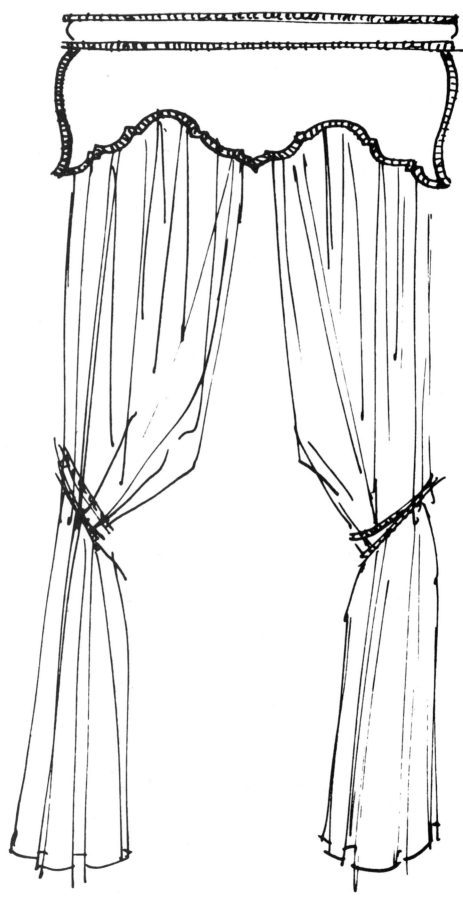

51

Queen Anne

52

Chippendale

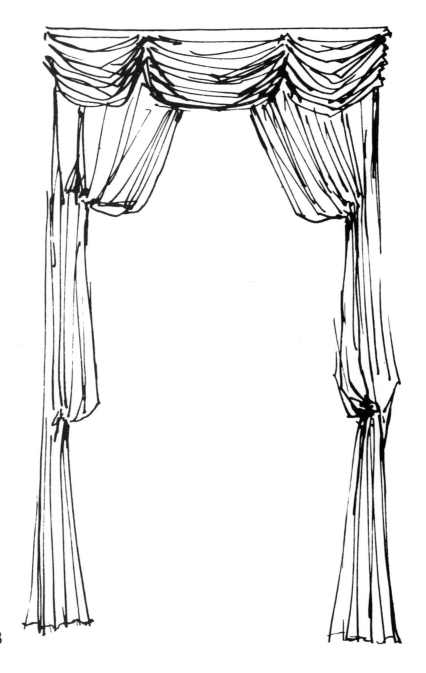

Chippendale

Chippendale

54

55

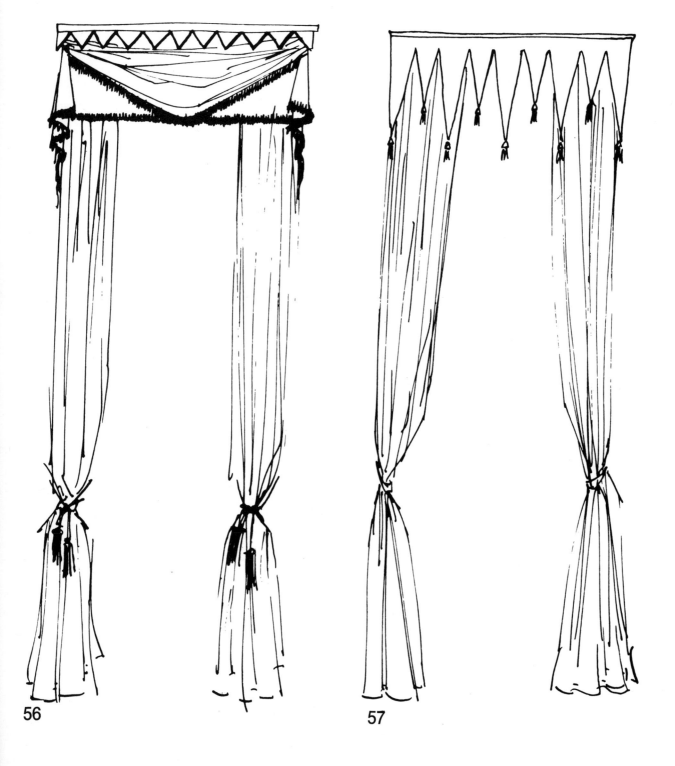

56

57

Adam

Adam

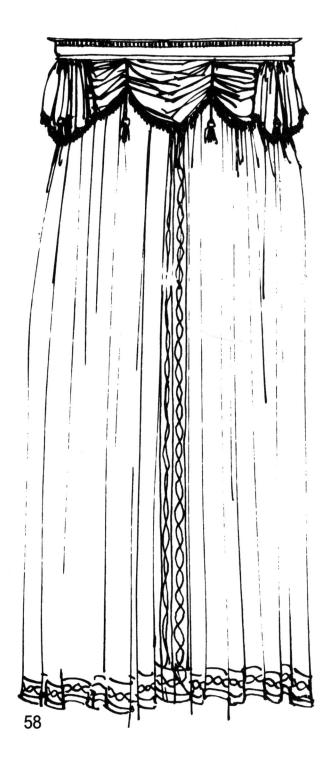

58

59

Regency

60

Regency

61

formal designs

metal medallions

62

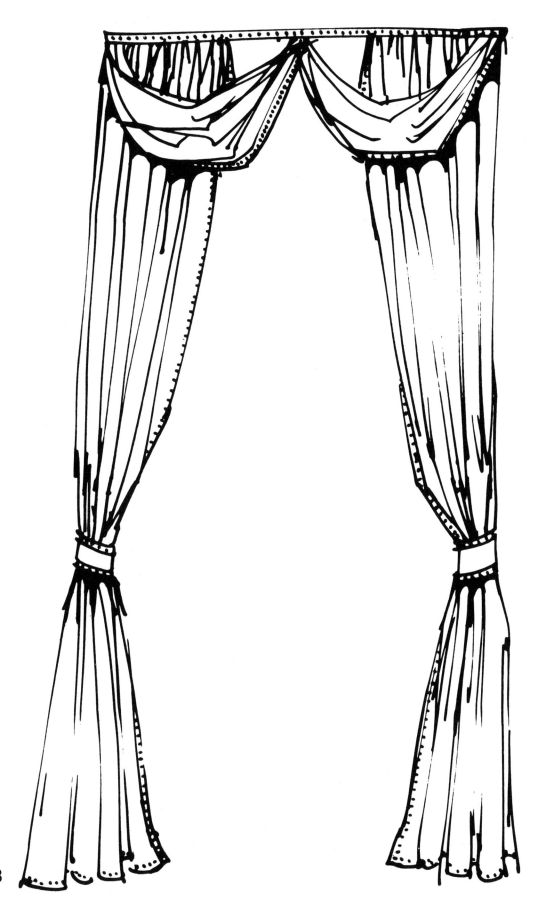

63

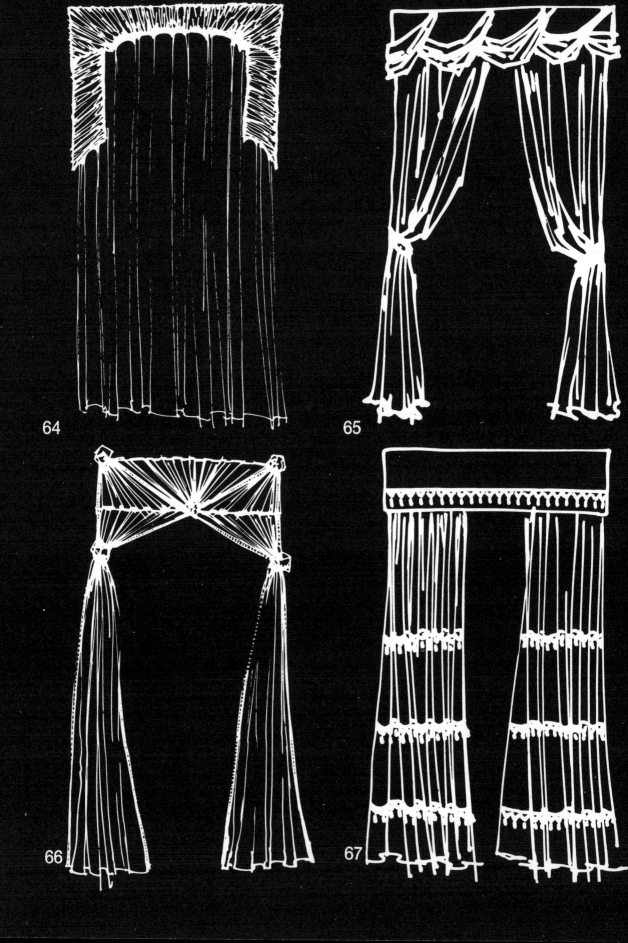

64

65

66

67

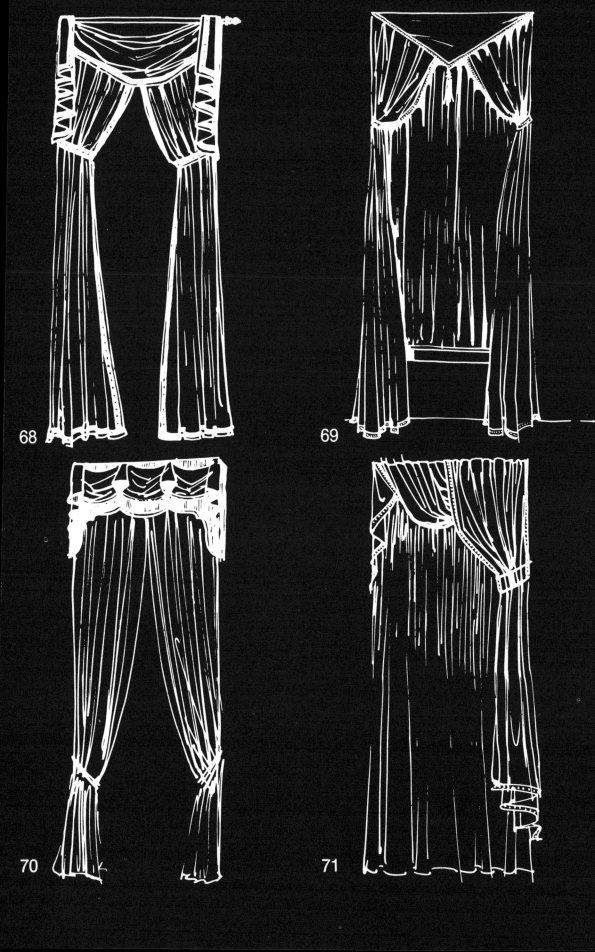

68

69

70

71

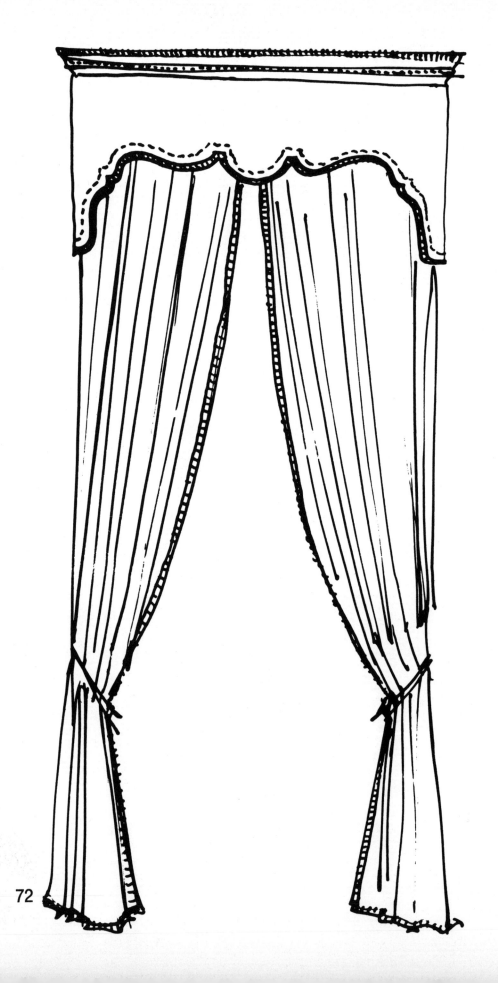

72

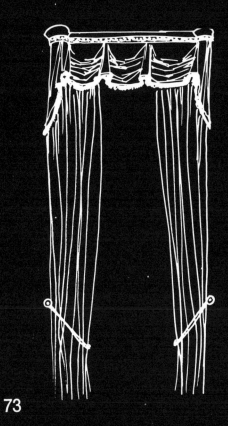

73

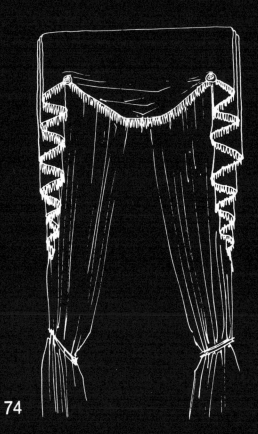

74

valance
and curtain
seem to be
one piece
drawn up
with loops
and drawstring

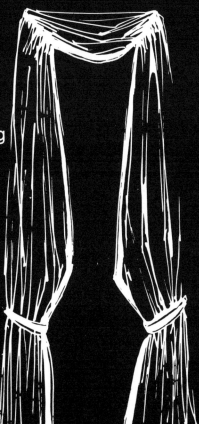

75

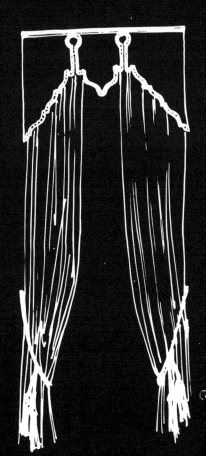

76

sheer curtains with
over panels of
heavier fabric

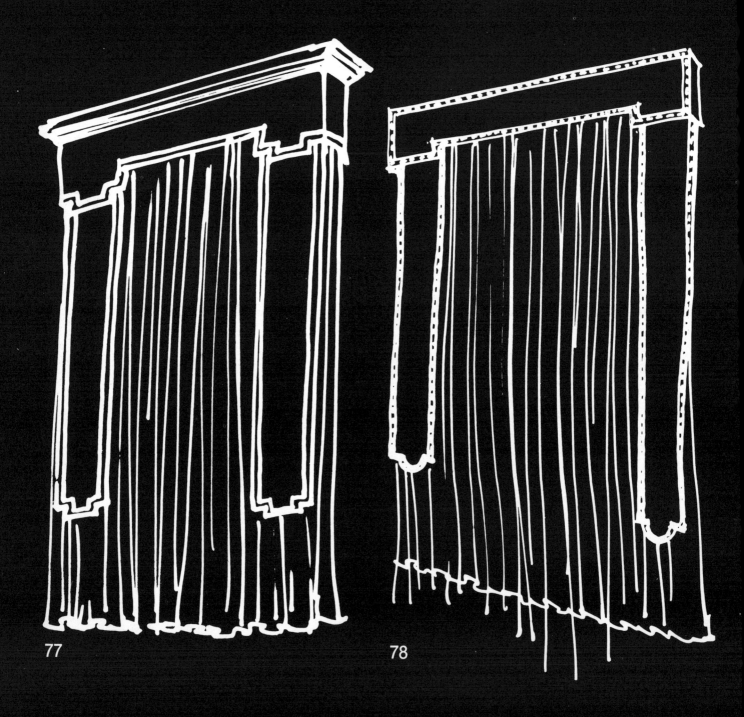

77   78

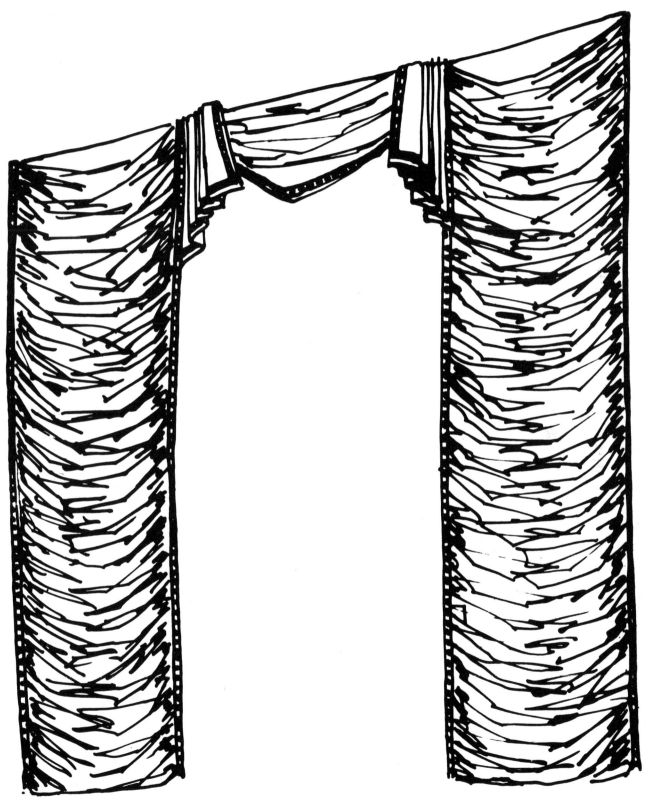

79

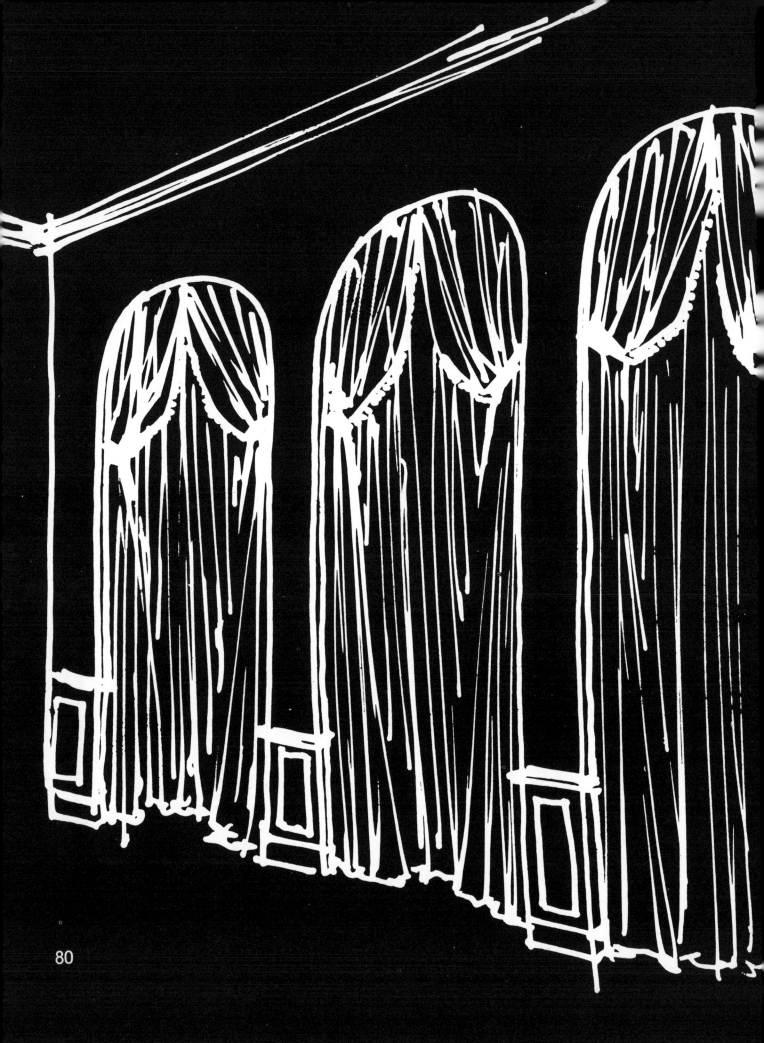

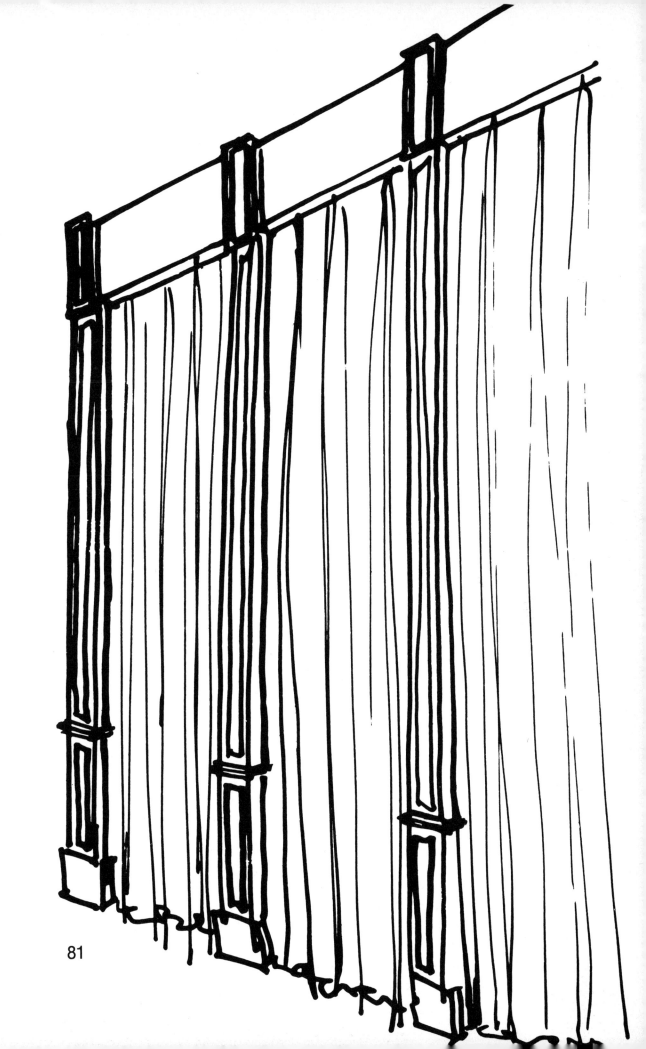

81

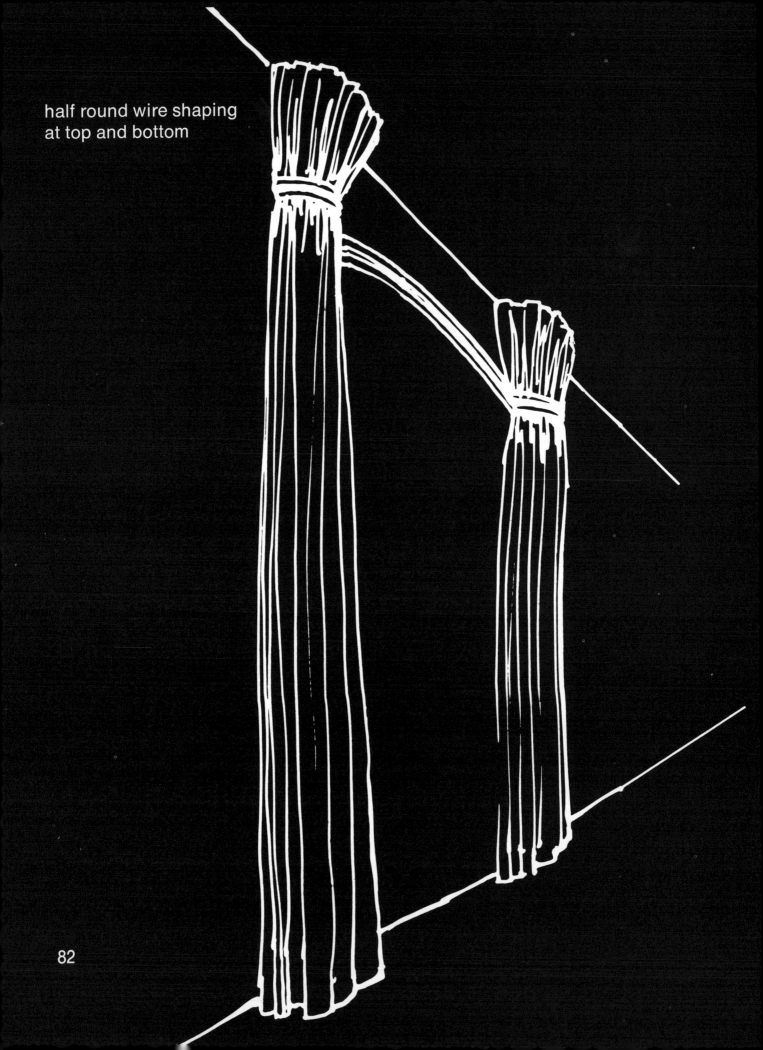

half round wire shaping
at top and bottom

82

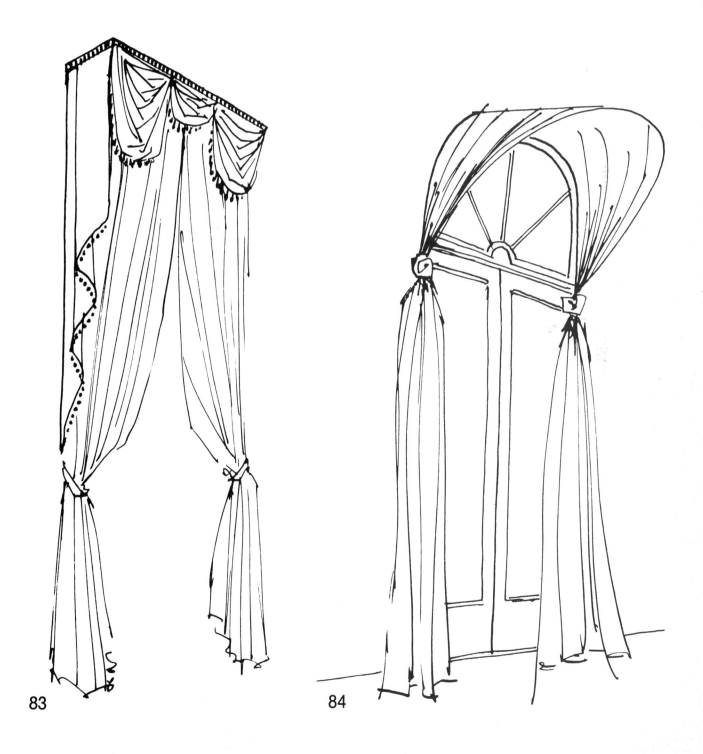

83

84

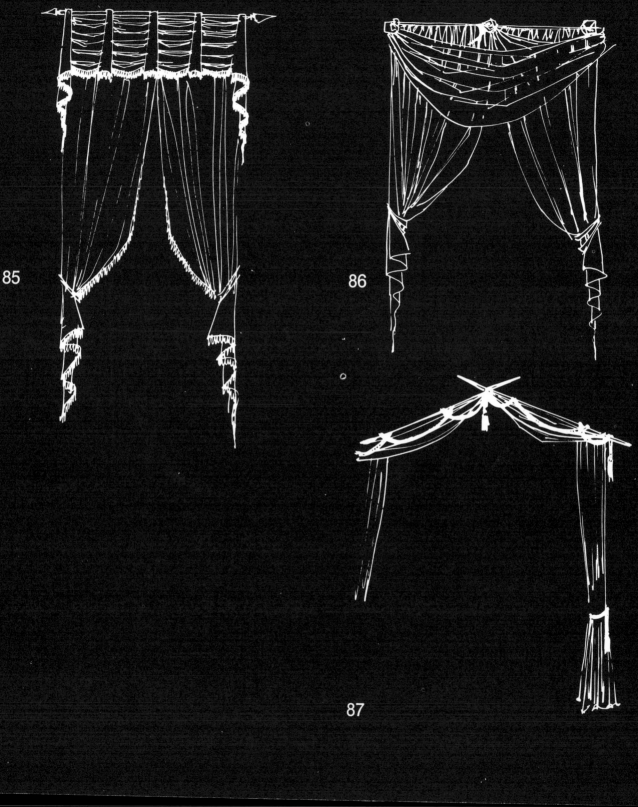

85

86

87

mirror panel
between two windows,
valance continuing over

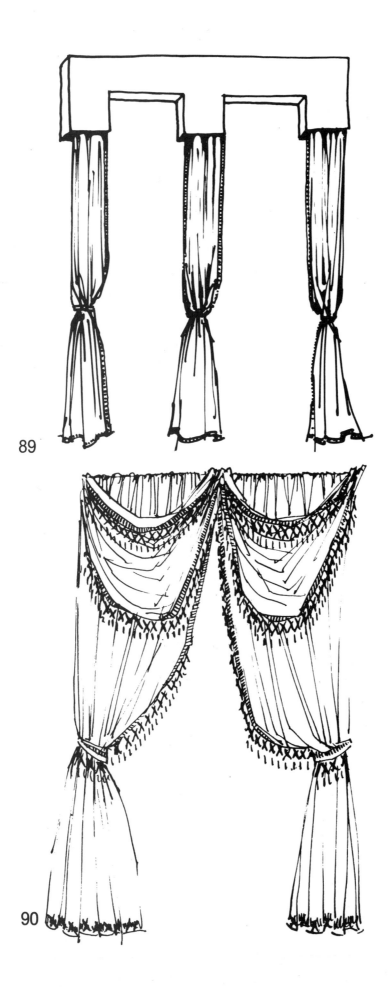

89

90

fabric rosettes

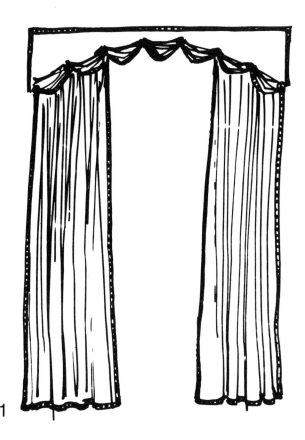

91

elaborate cornice and
curtains in "trompe l'oeil"
with real undercurtains

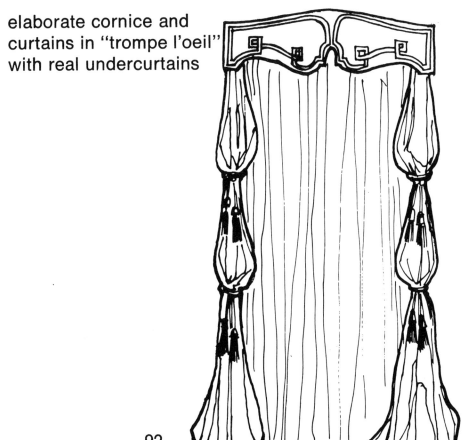

92

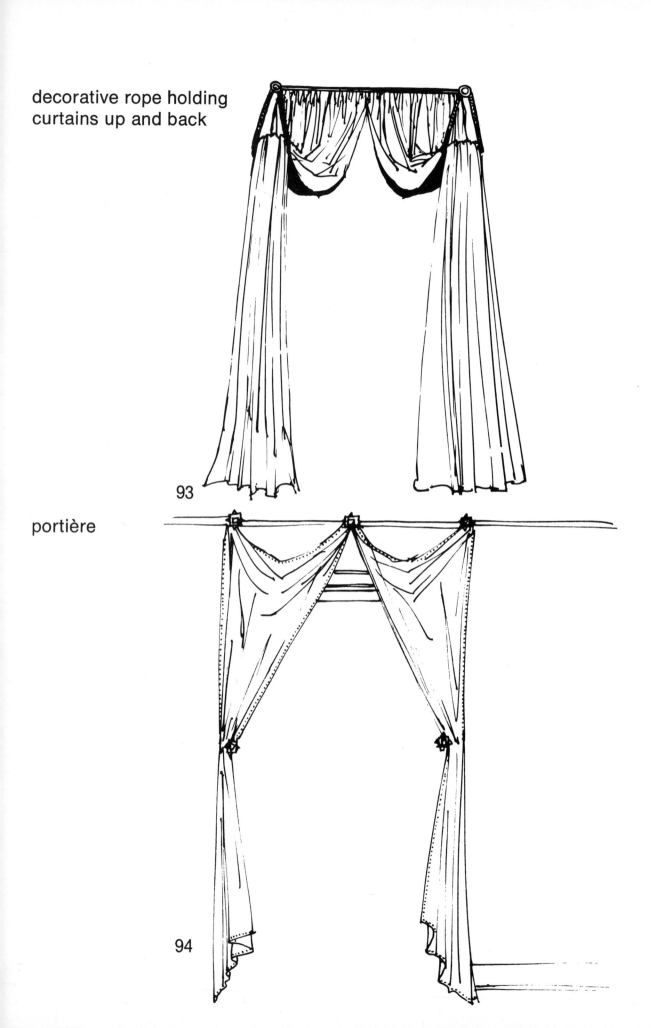

decorative rope holding
curtains up and back

93

portière

94

tie poles with cord

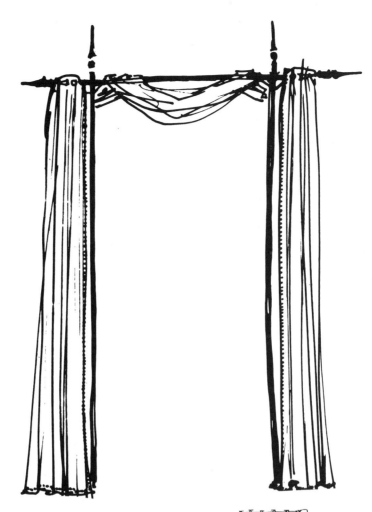

95

valance behind
curtains
and covered rod

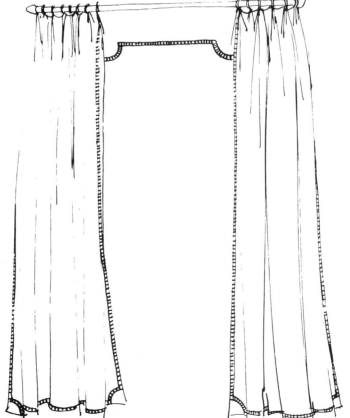

96

97

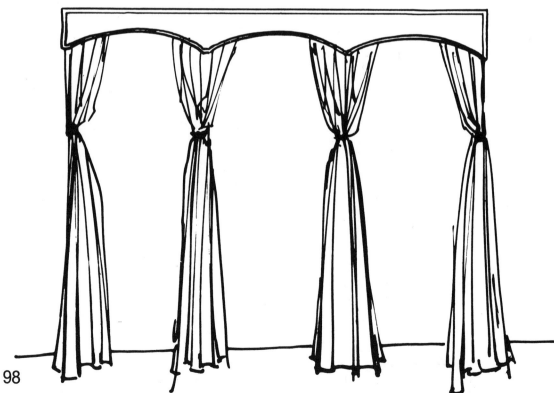

98

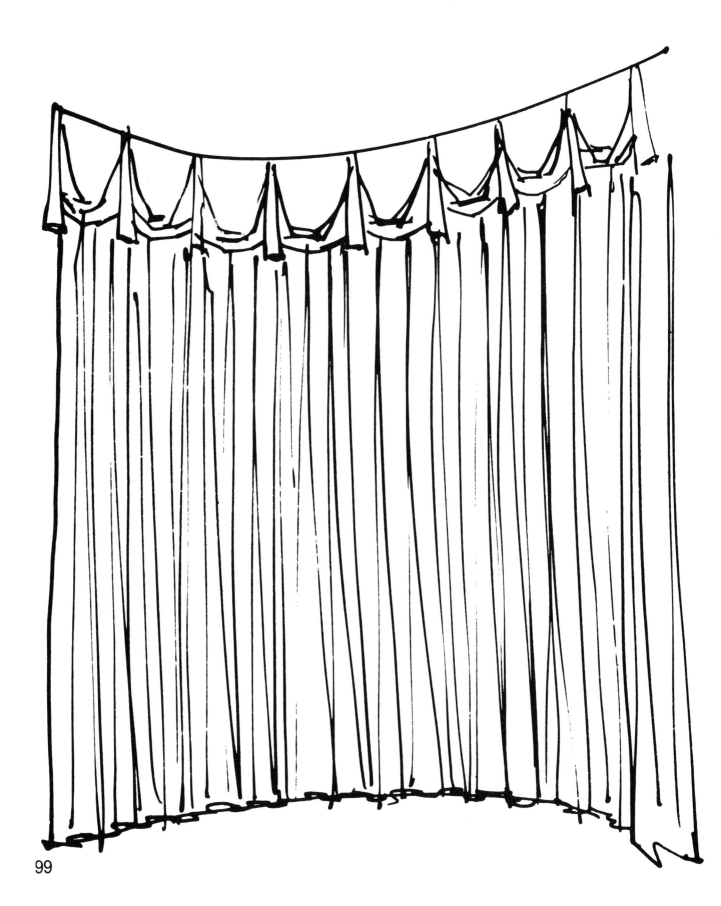

99

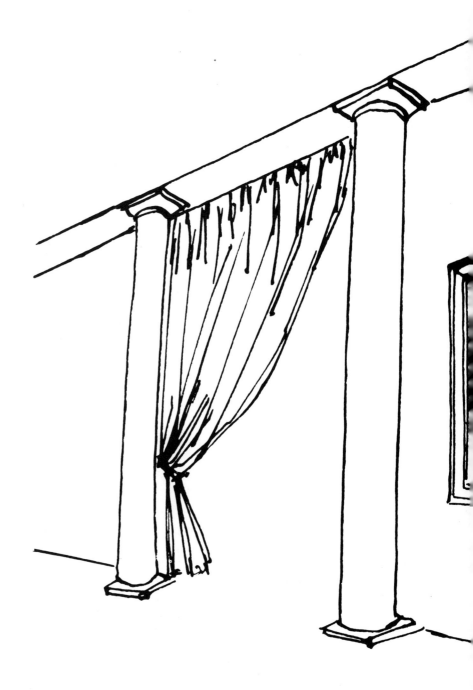

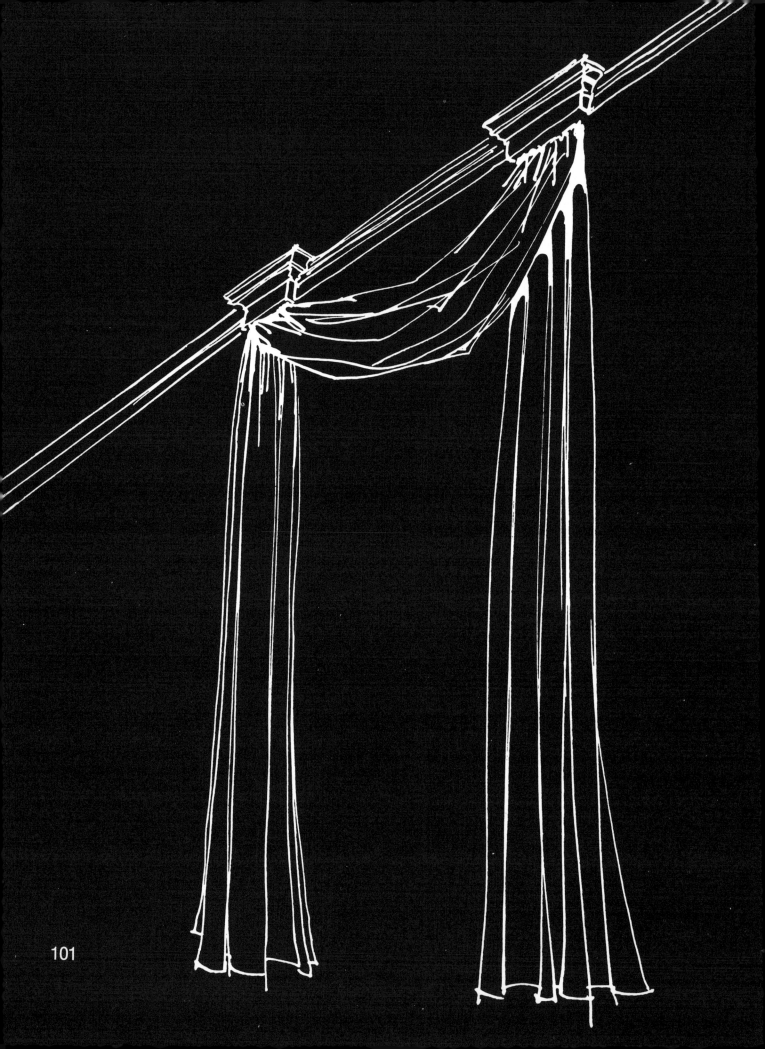

cords and tassels

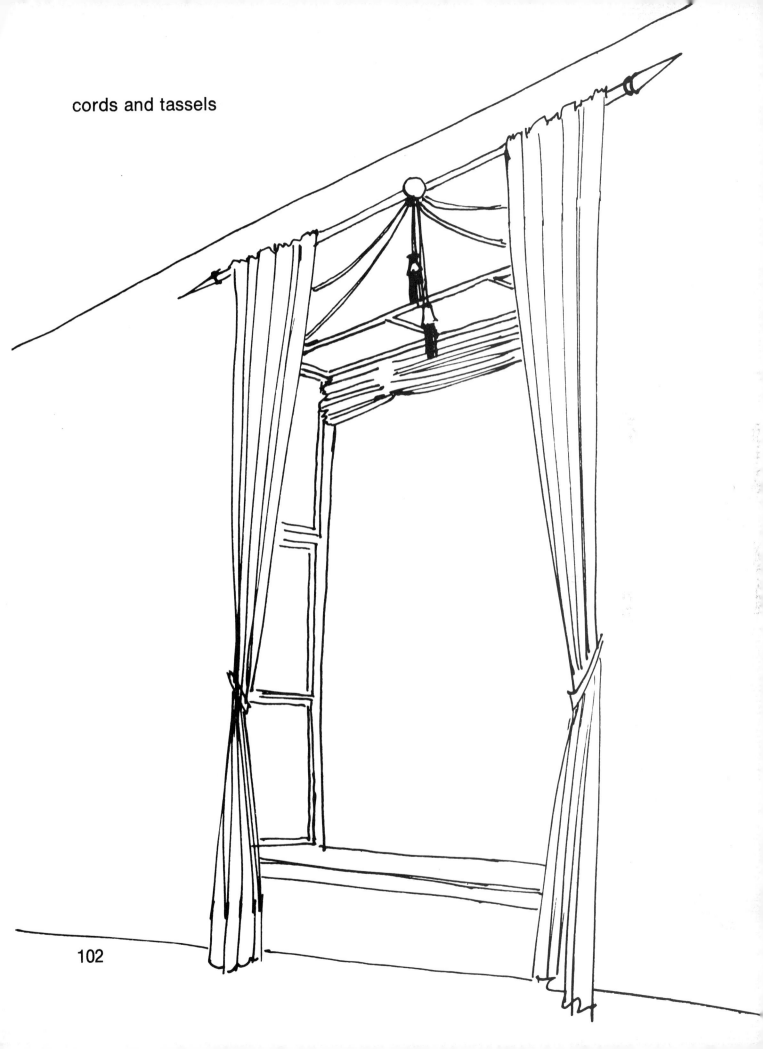

French door
treatment
allowing doors
to open

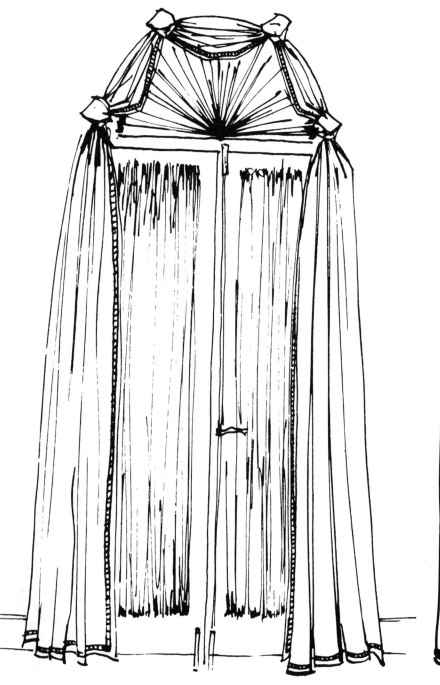

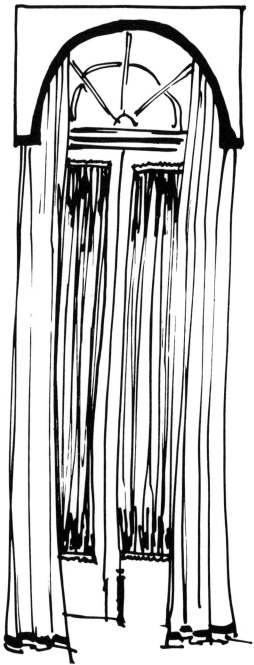

103

104

curtains hanging
on doors
for easy passage

shell cornice

105

106

vertical stripes on
curtains,
diagonal on swags

drapery panels
swagged at edge
and drawn back with a
cord running through rings

107

108

two fabrics,
print for lining
and tie-backs

metal grill inserted at
top of arch,
curtains installed behind,
or sheer curtains installed
in front

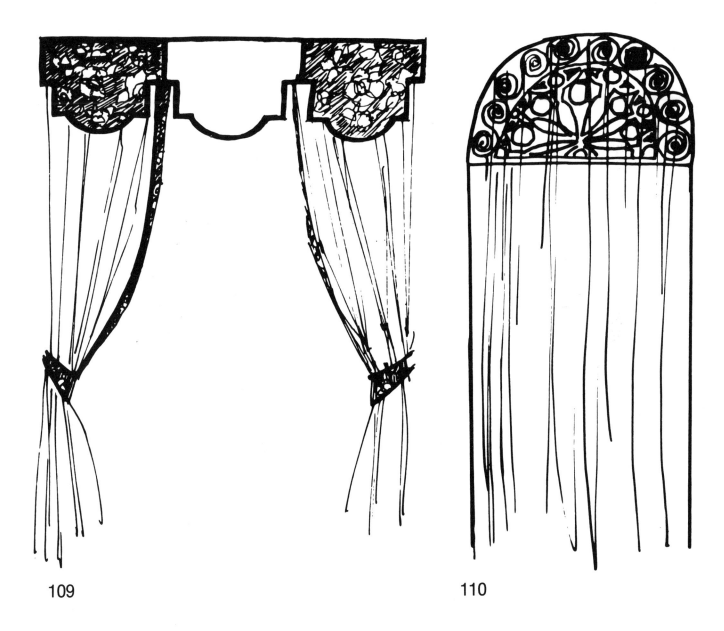

109

110

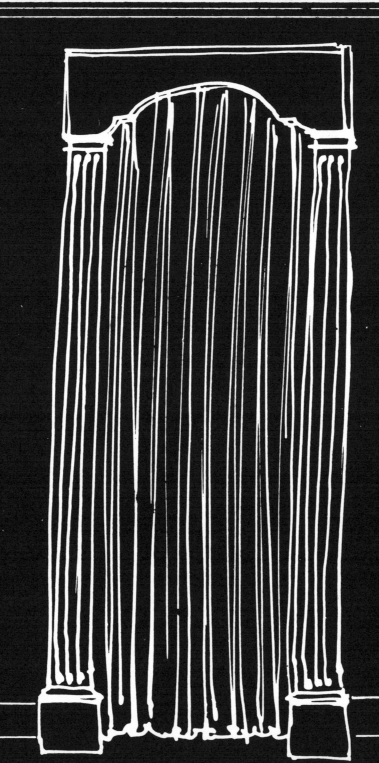

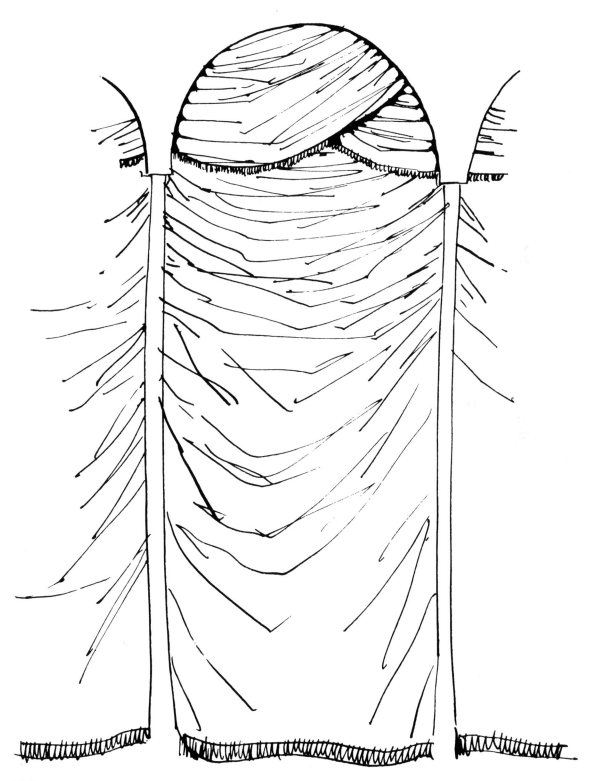

112

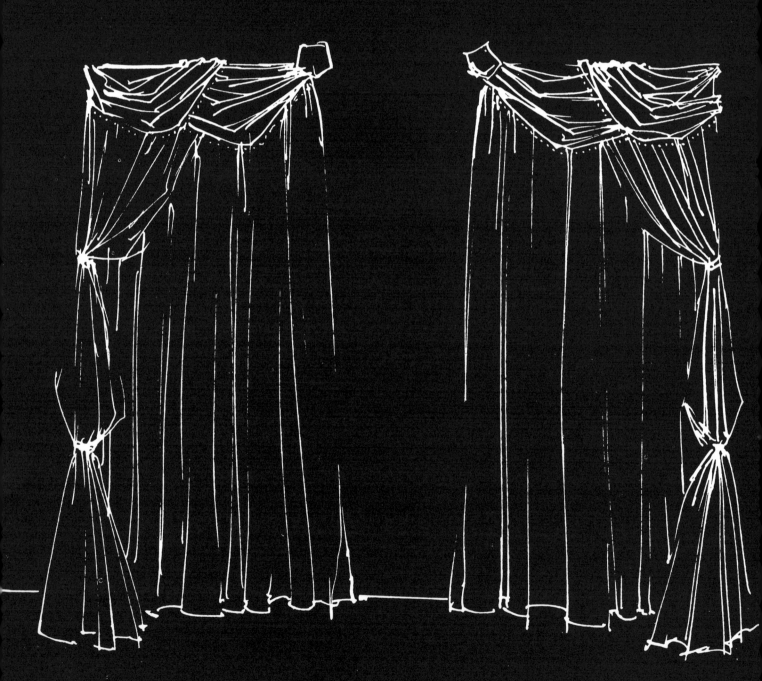

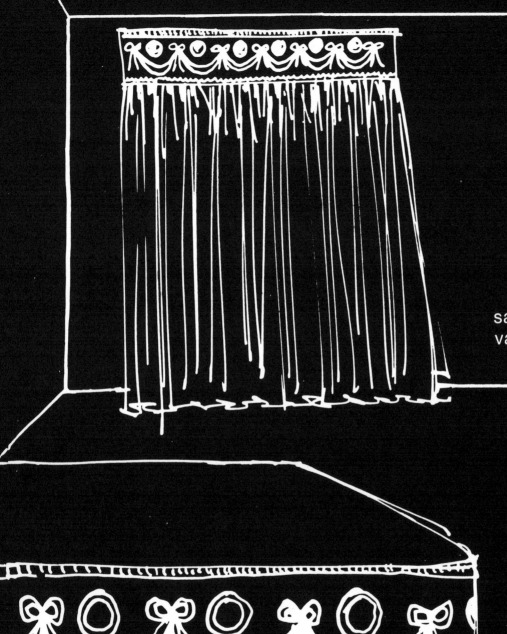

same fabric on
valance and spread

115

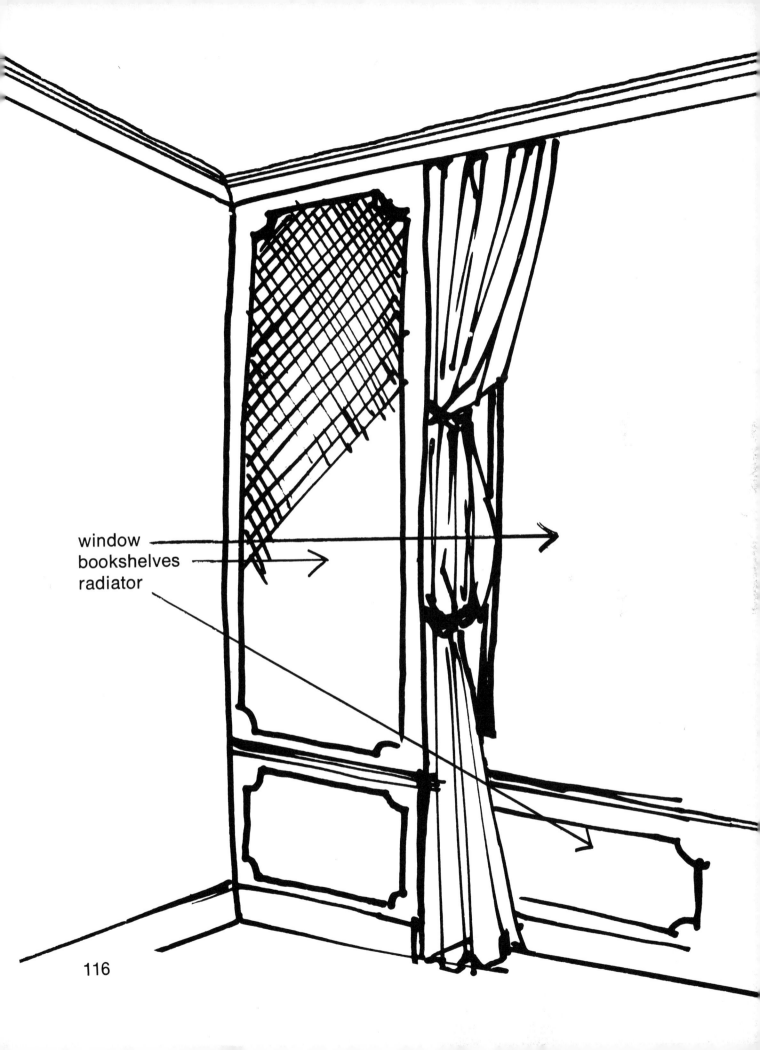

window
bookshelves
radiator

116

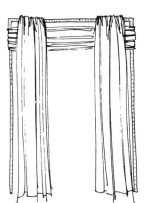

casual
designs

decorative tapes
attached
to ceiling,
terminating
in tassels

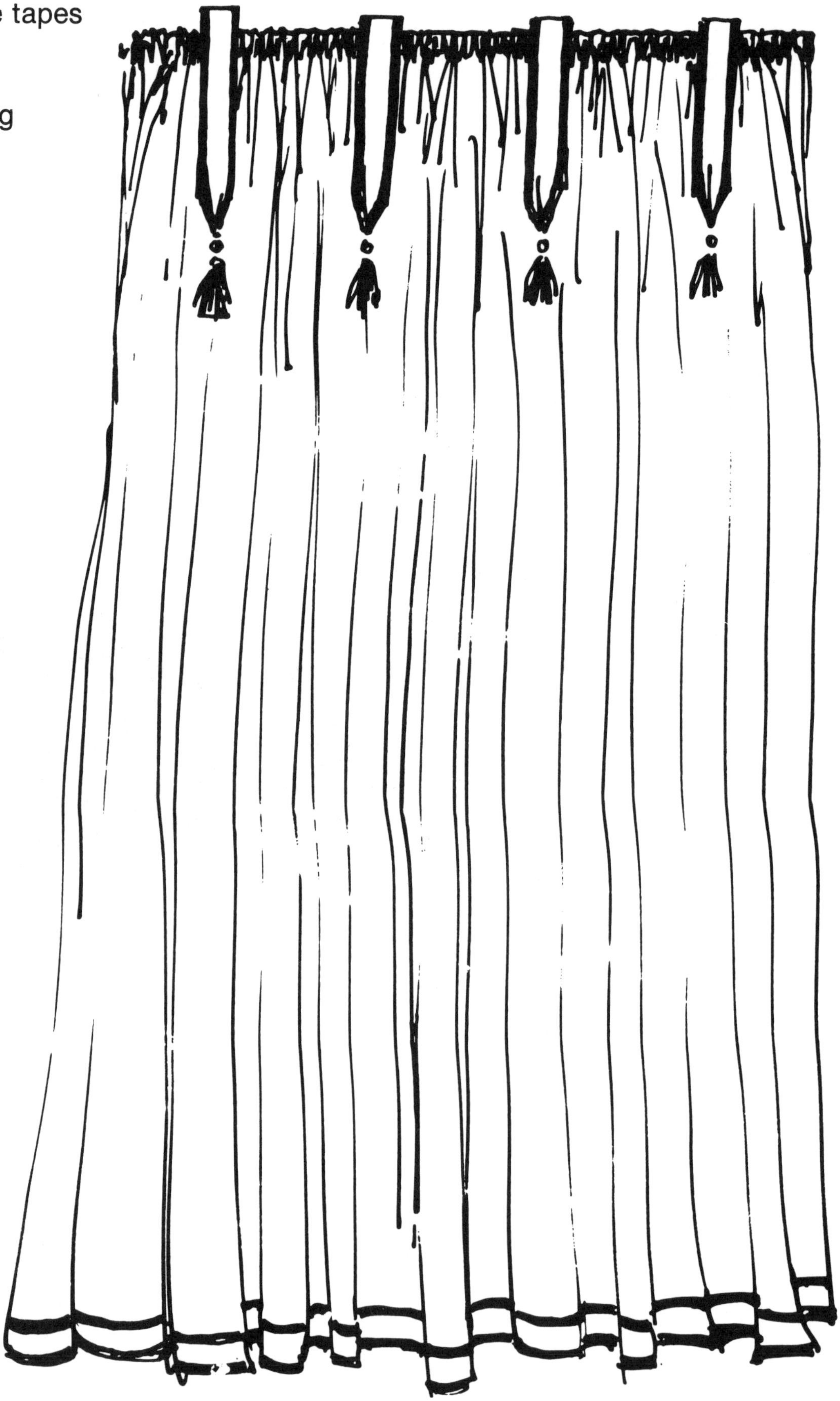

117

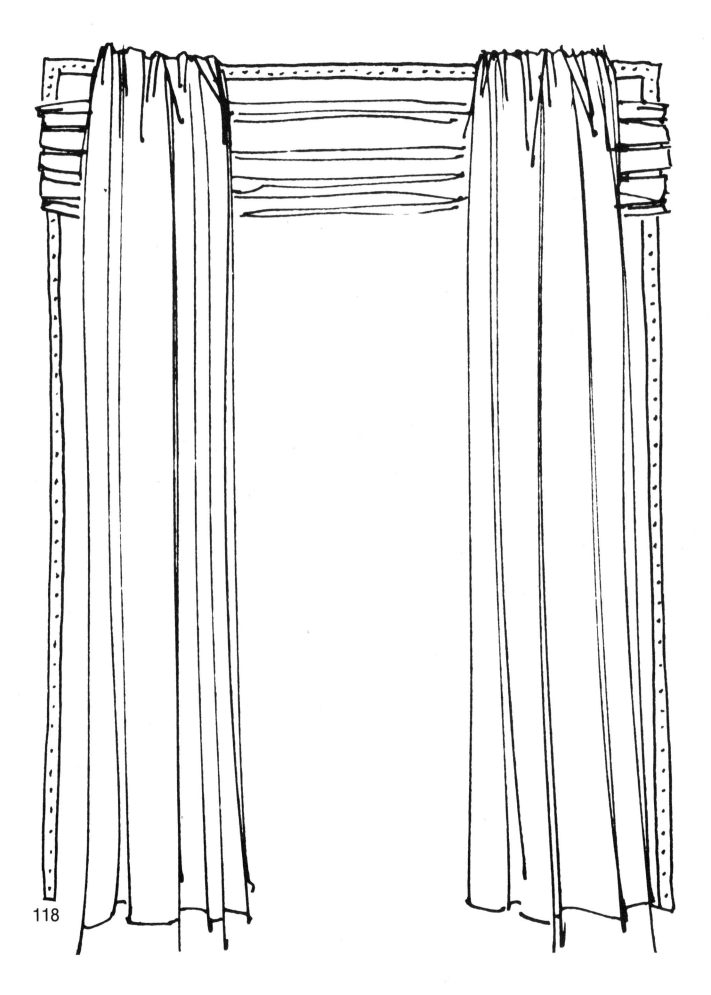

sheer curtains
in front of swag valance

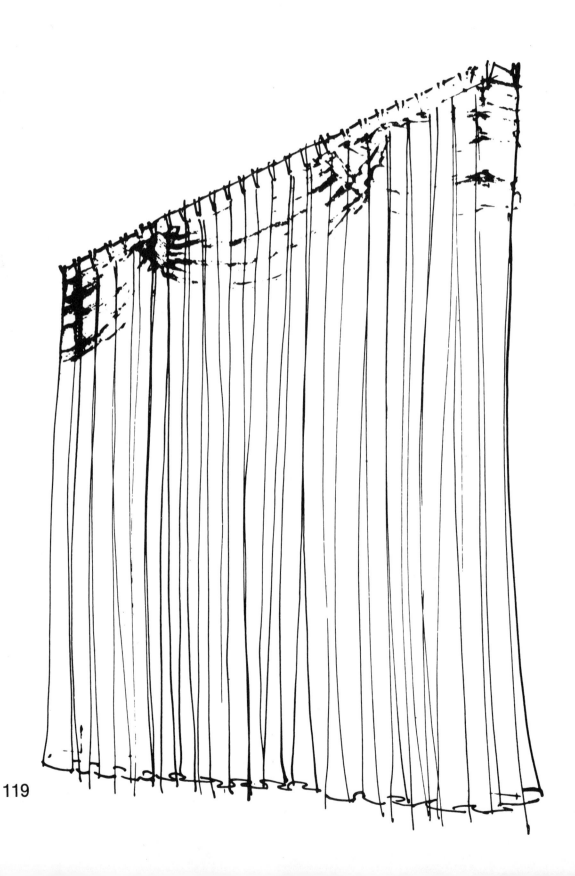

119

metal grill

120

121

open frame
with hanging tassels

open bamboo design

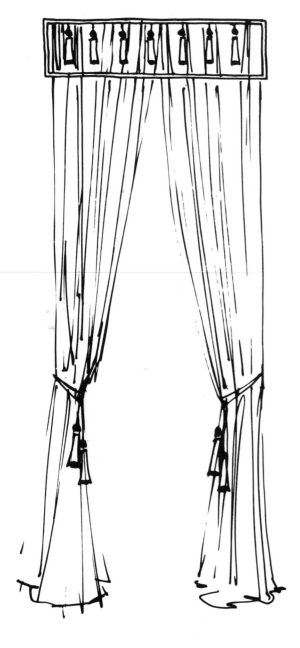

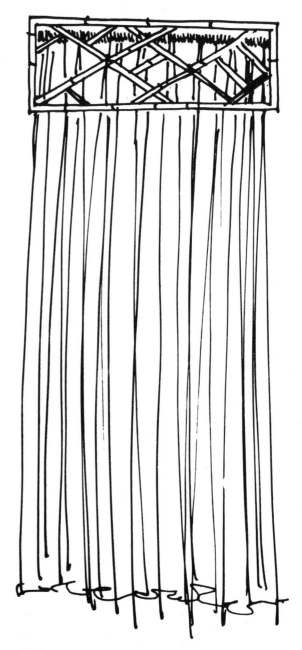

122

123

fabric-covered wooden frame
with curtains inside

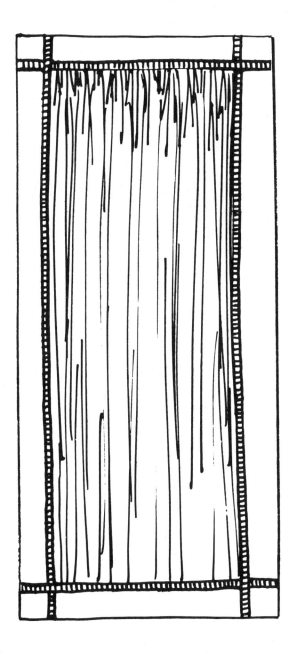

124

125

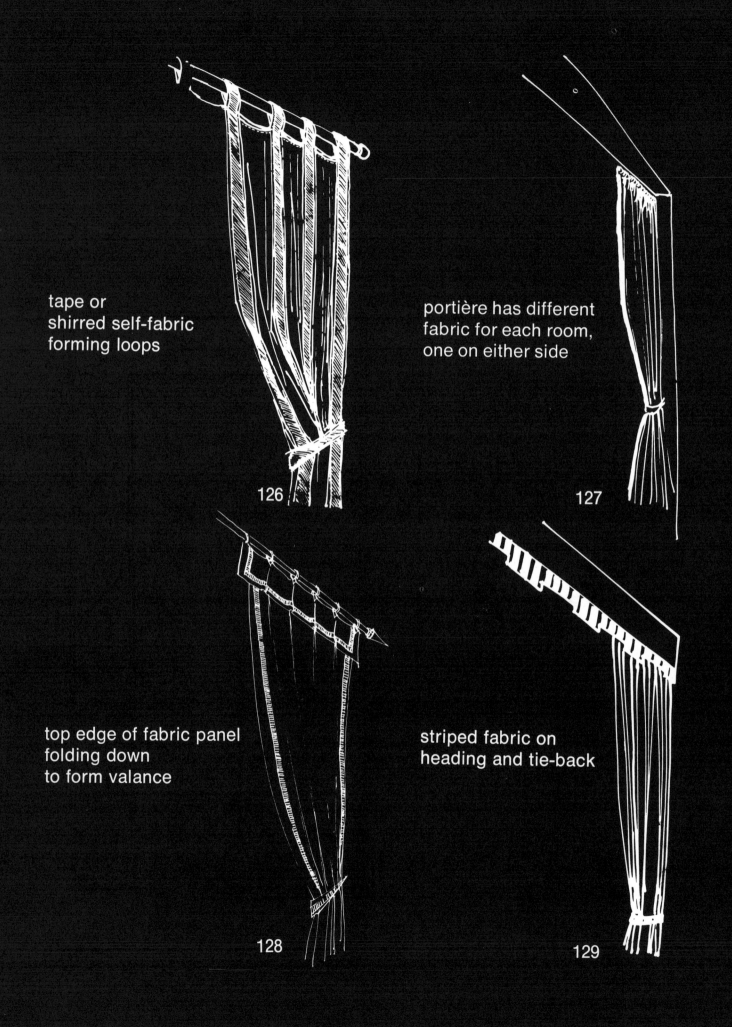

tape or
shirred self-fabric
forming loops

portière has different
fabric for each room,
one on either side

126

127

top edge of fabric panel
folding down
to form valance

striped fabric on
heading and tie-back

128

129

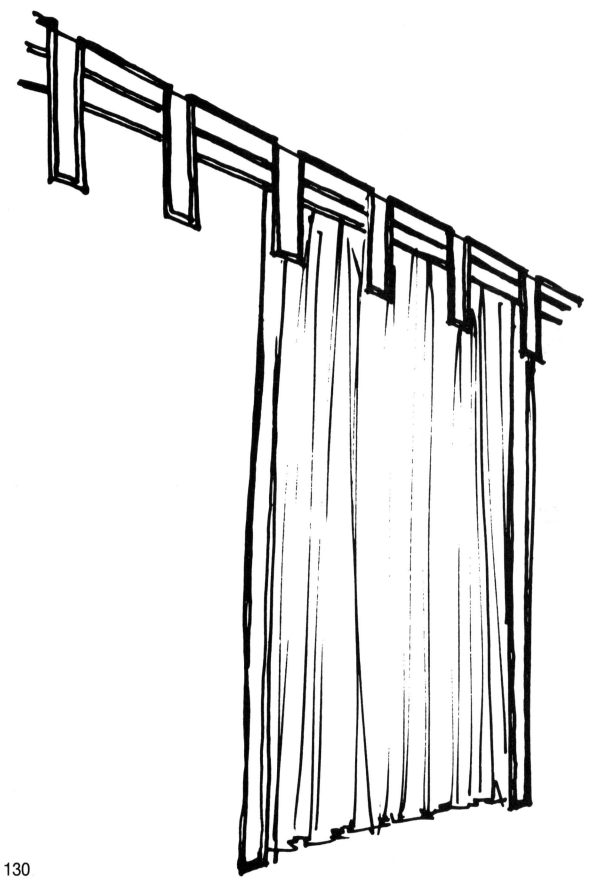

130

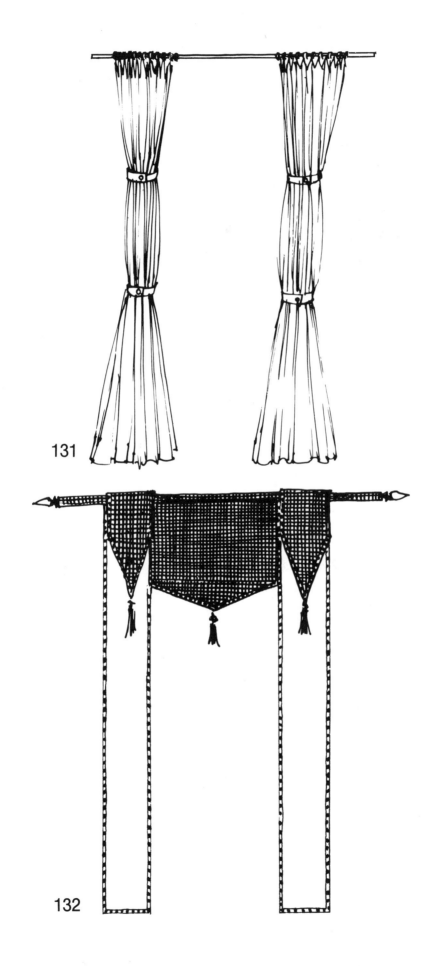

131

132

leather treatment

welt
fringe
buckles

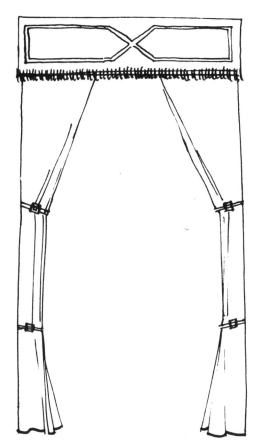

133

flat, pressed pleats
for curtains
and heading

134

bay window
with lowered ceiling

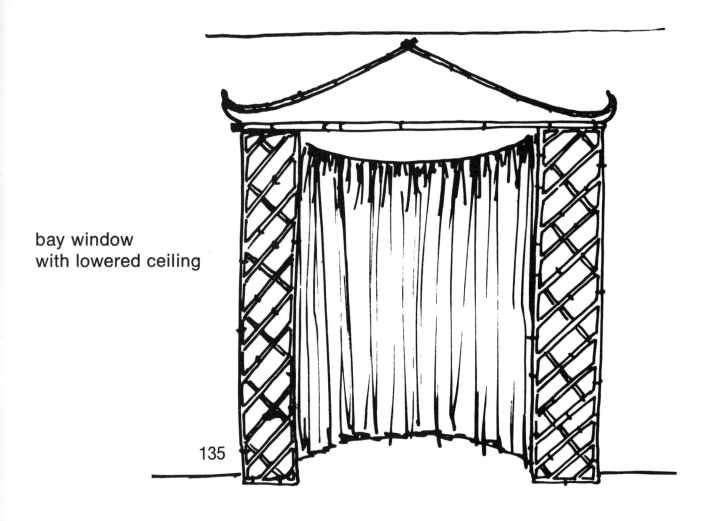

135

heavy wood beams
forming
architectural treatment

136

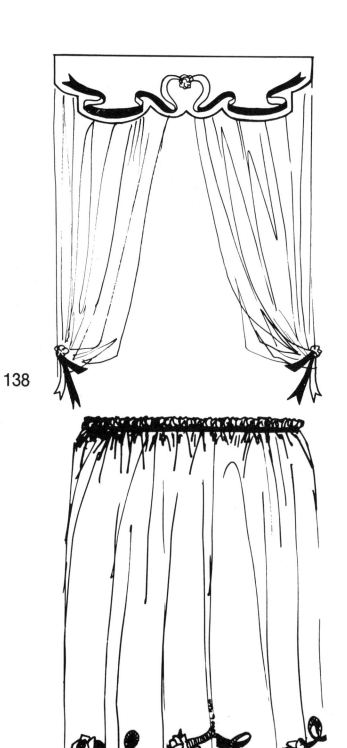

138

139

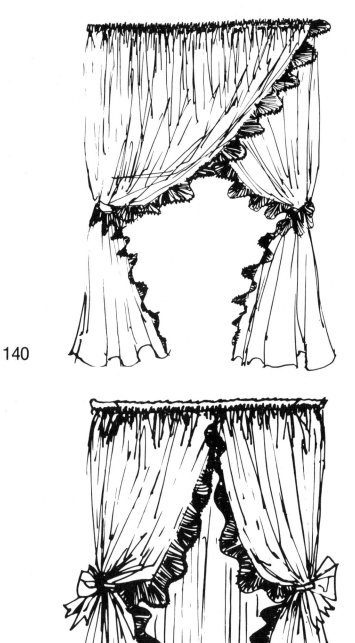

140

141

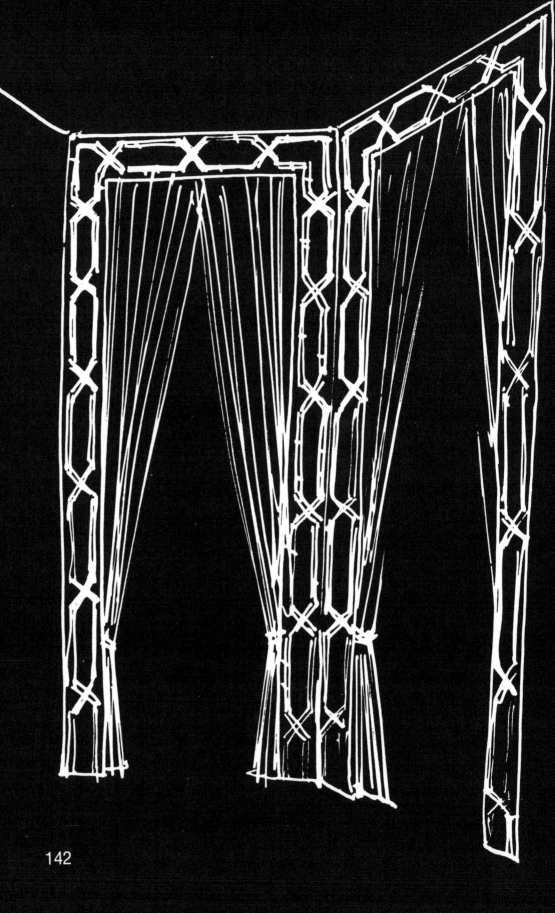

142

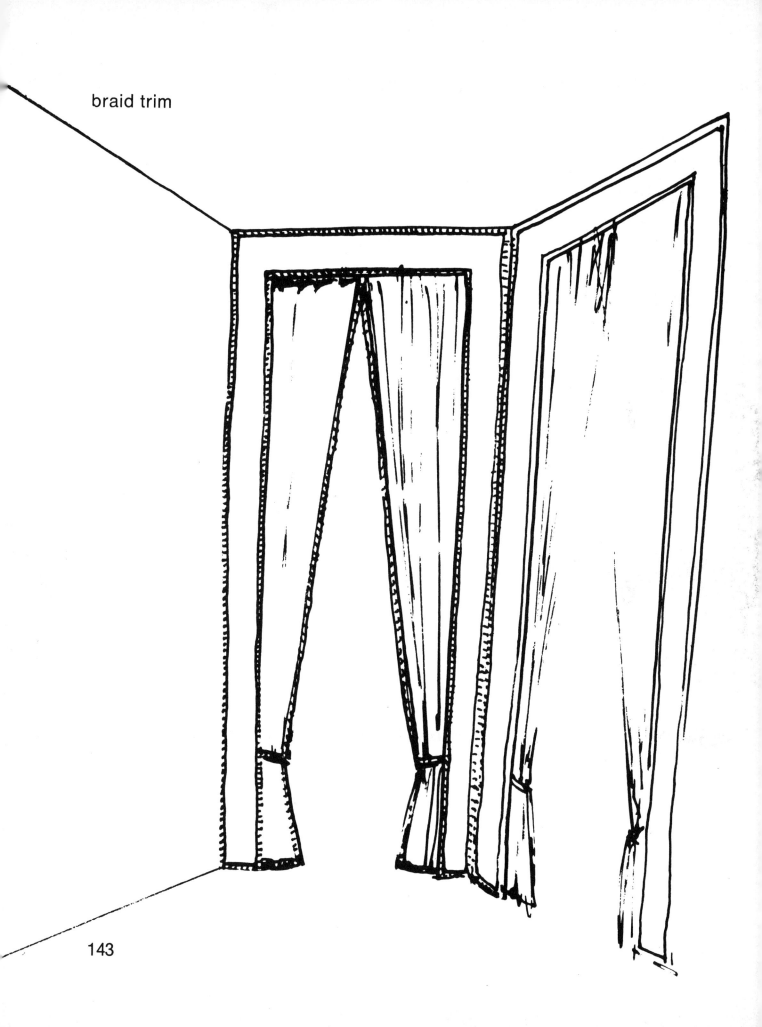

braid trim

143

bay window
arches with sheer white curtains,
print or colored fabric above

flowered wallpaper border

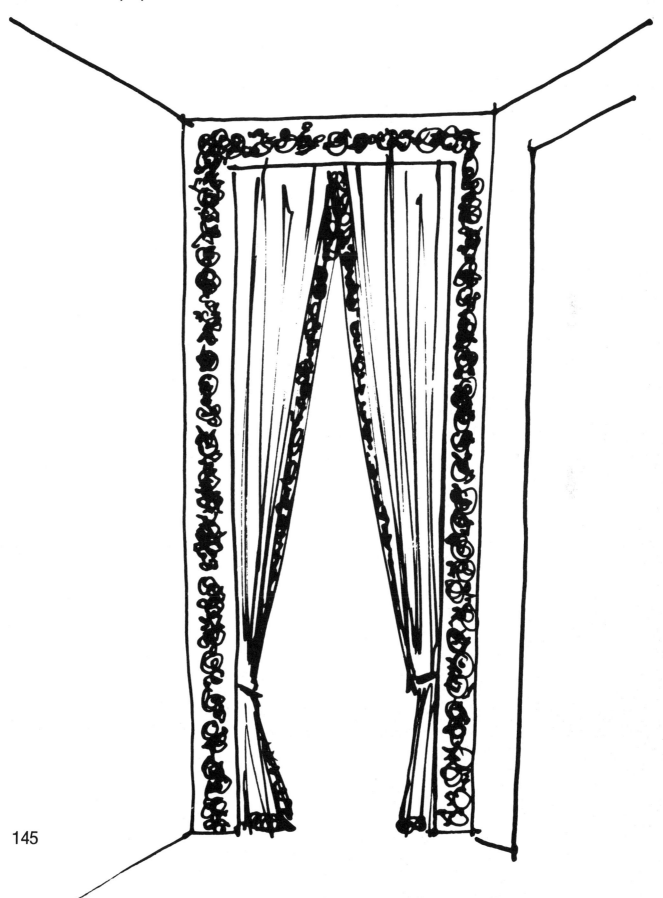

145

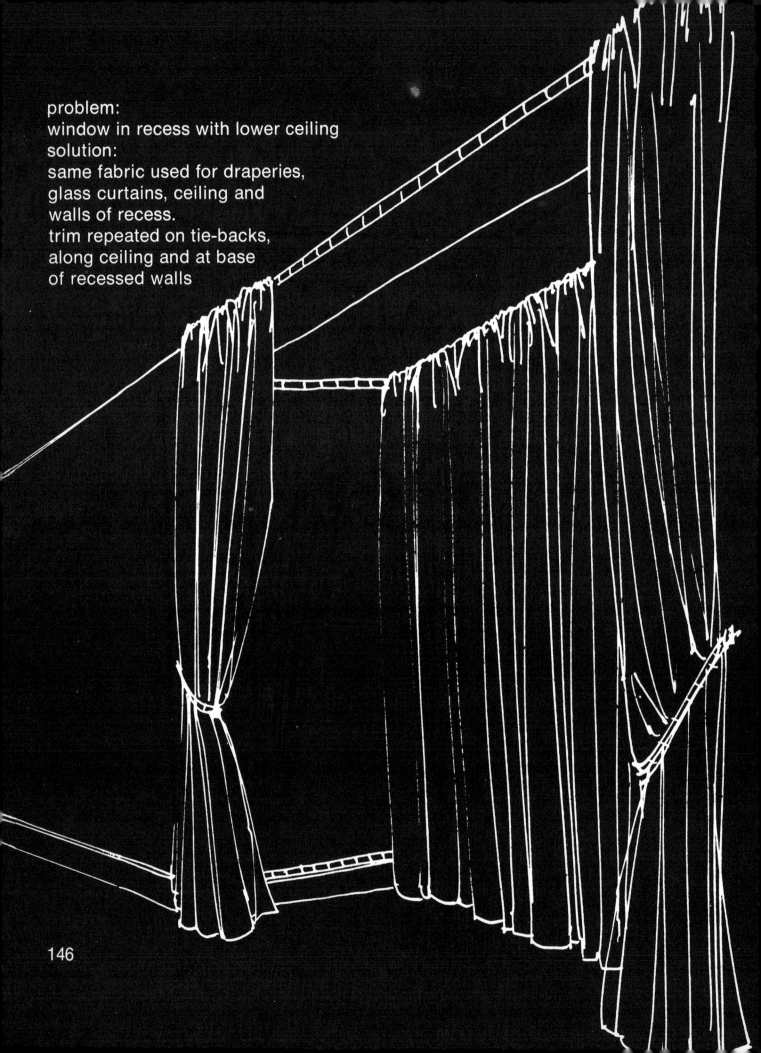

problem:
window in recess with lower ceiling
solution:
same fabric used for draperies,
glass curtains, ceiling and
walls of recess.
trim repeated on tie-backs,
along ceiling and at base
of recessed walls

146

building column
bookshelves
new "wall"

147

148

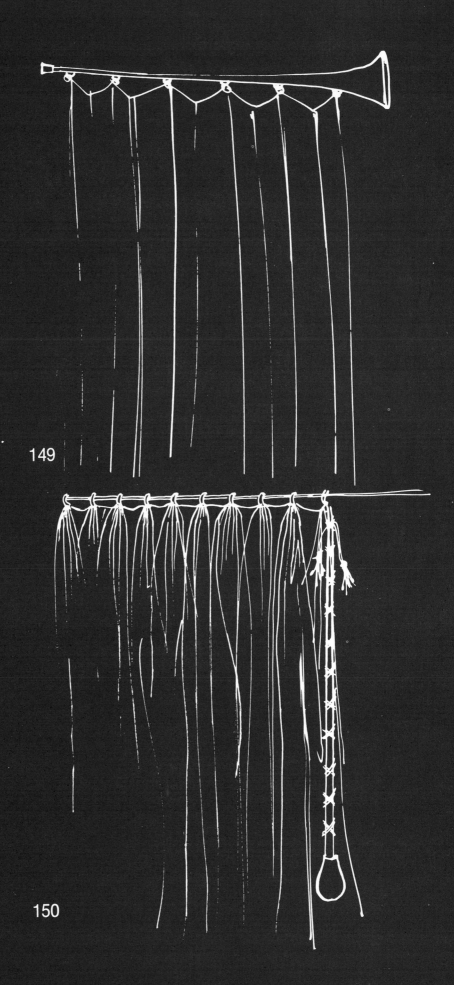

149

150

half-round columns
covered with
Persian style paper
or fabric

151

target valance and
score shade
for boy's room
or recreation room

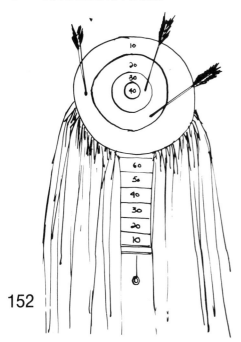

152

metal curtain hanging
on spear or halberd

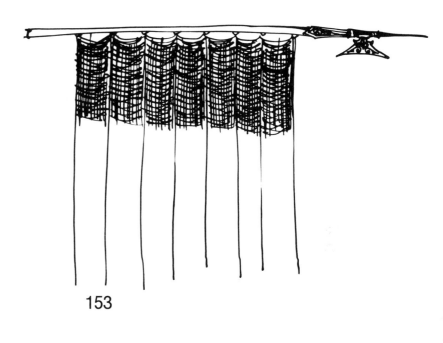

153

bandanas
knotted to rings

four bandanas

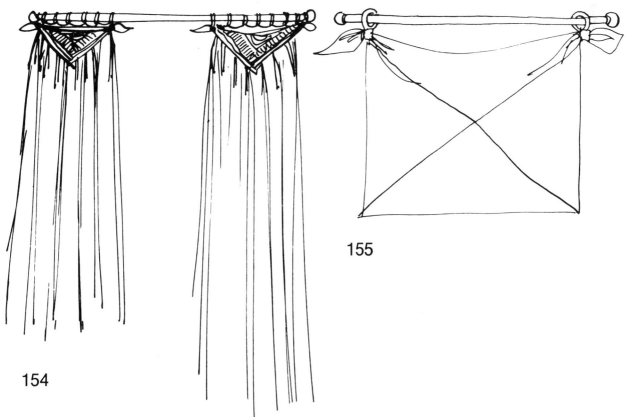

154

155

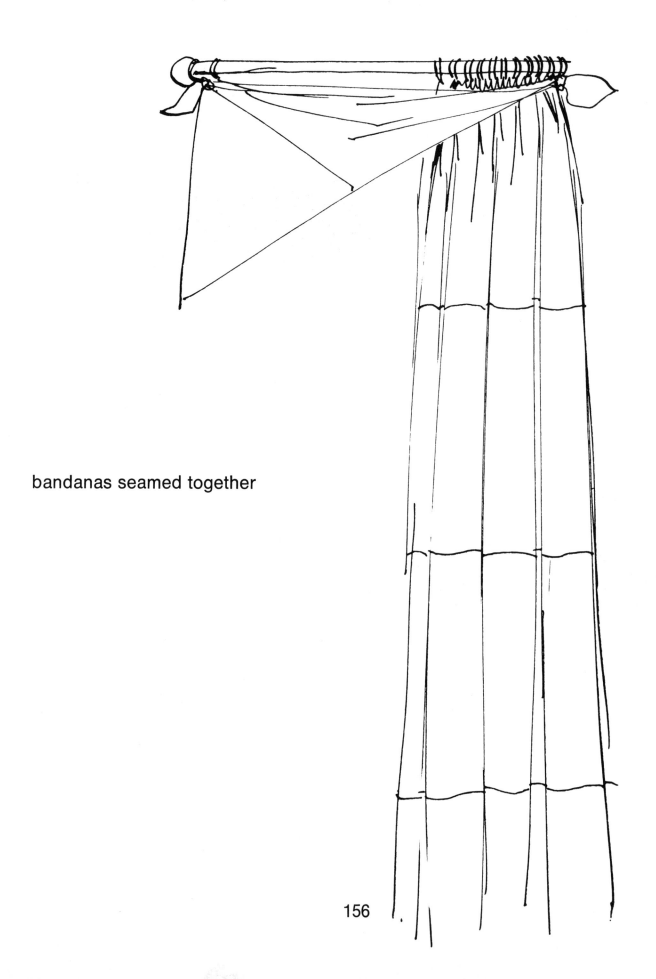

bandanas seamed together

156

print lining
casually exposed
on tie-back draperies

157

dormer window
interior awning

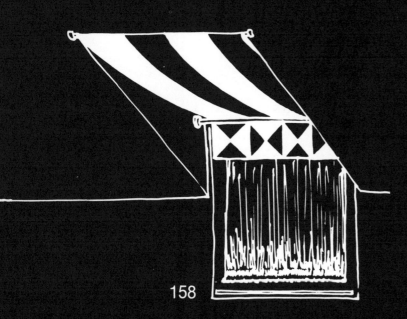

158

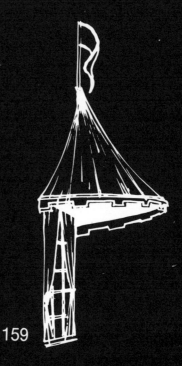

159

bamboo rod
with tassel of
unraveled rope

two fabrics

pull-up shade
of bold colored
striped fabric
on wooden roll bar
between
two stationary
straight panels
in black and white

160

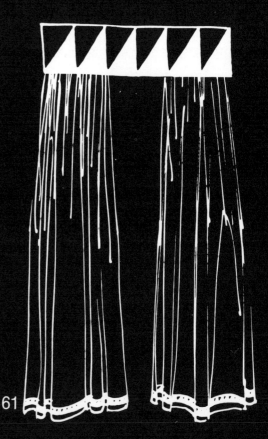

161

"blockhead"
shapes 2 inches thick
covered with different colored felt
and applied to wall

single remaining shape
after child is mature

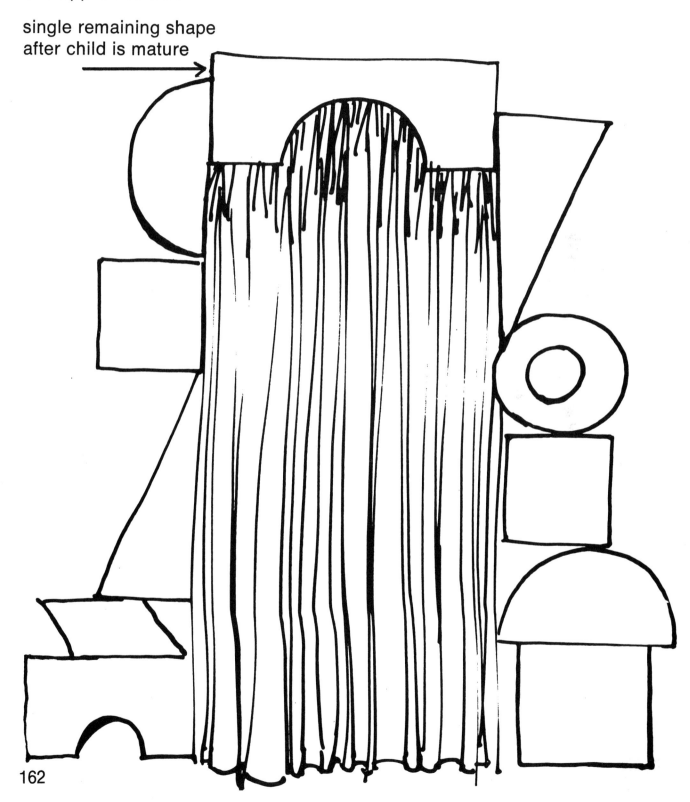

wooden frame

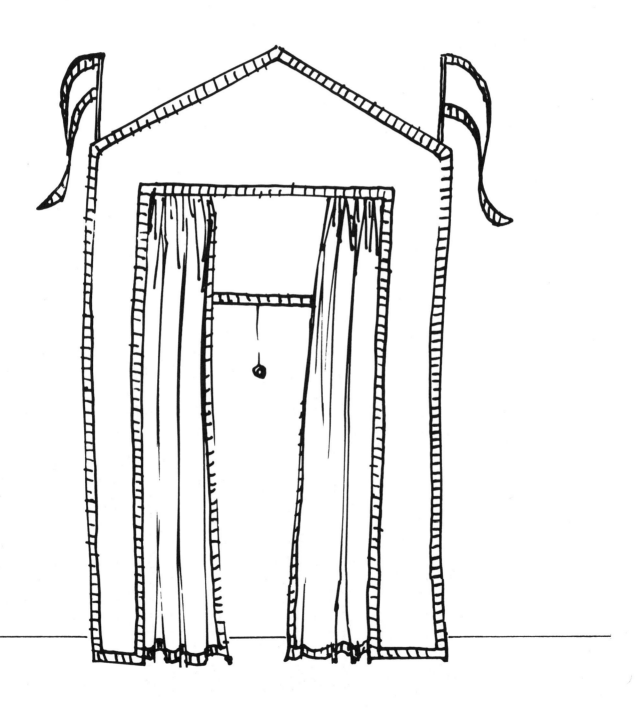

bold patterned fabric
panels on each side

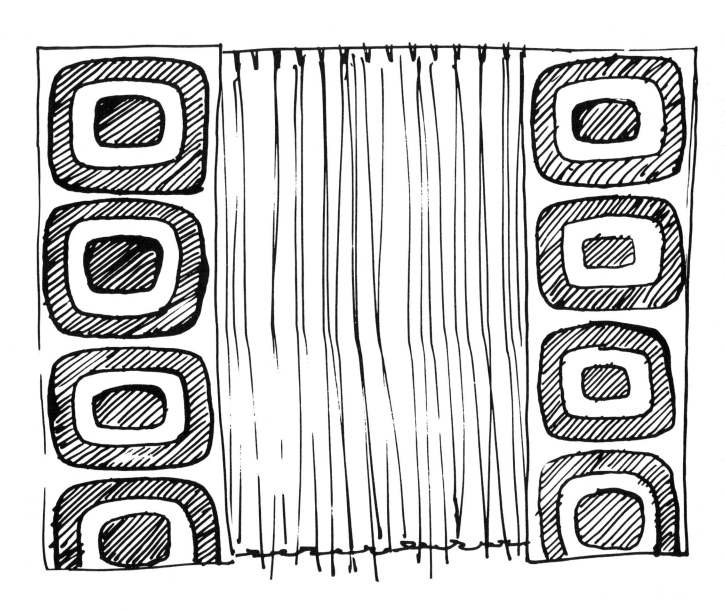

brass brackets

165

166

sheer curtain
for high window

167

168

side   front

169

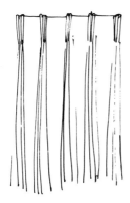 headings

French

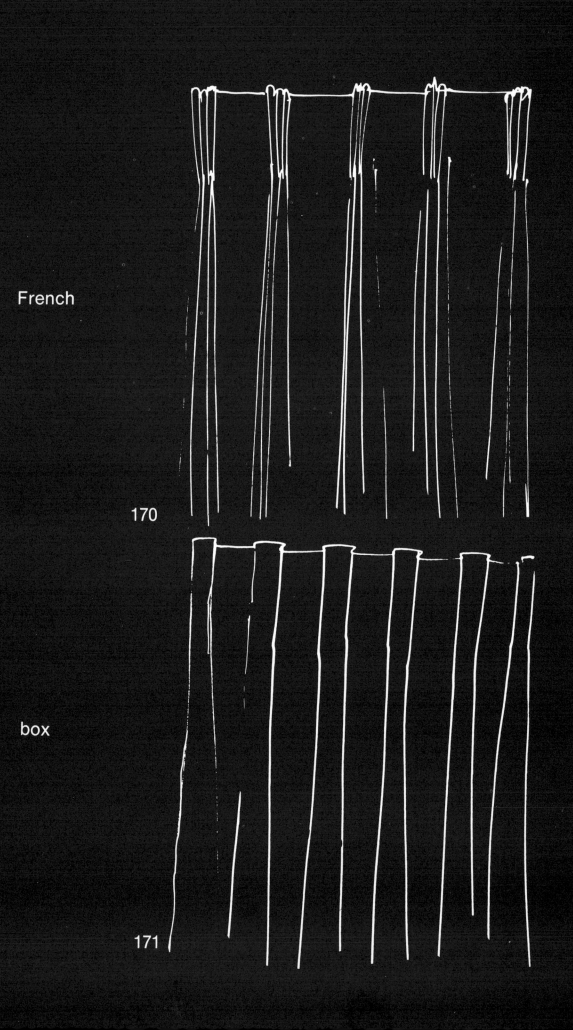

170

box

171

French with rings

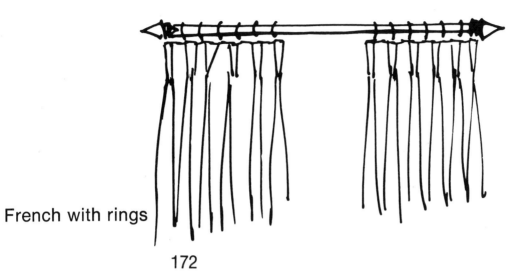

172

double shirring

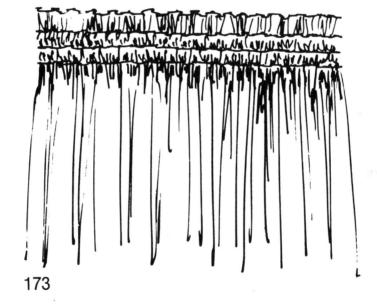

173

shirred pocket

174

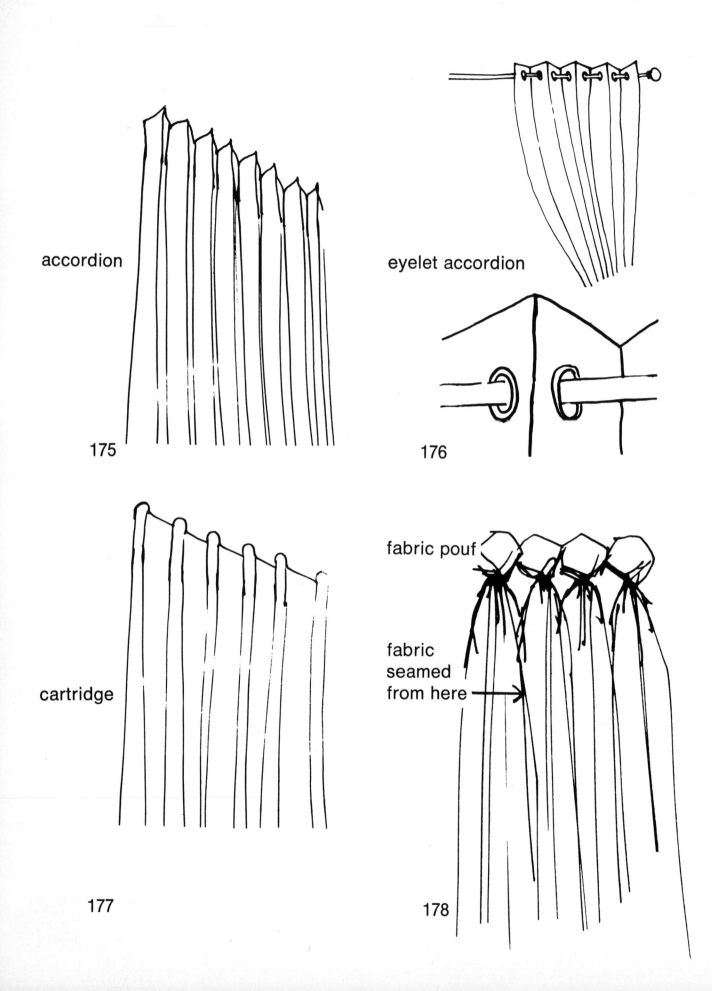

accordion

175

eyelet accordion

176

cartridge

177

fabric pouf

fabric
seamed
from here

178

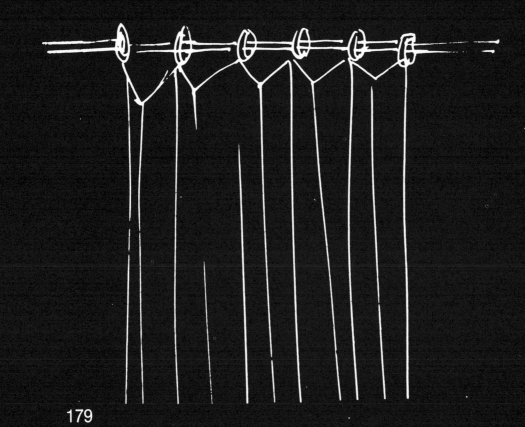

cafe

179

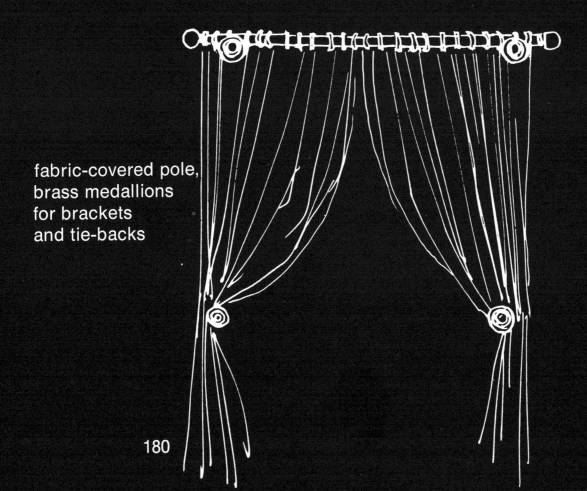

fabric-covered pole,
brass medallions
for brackets
and tie-backs

180

tie-backs

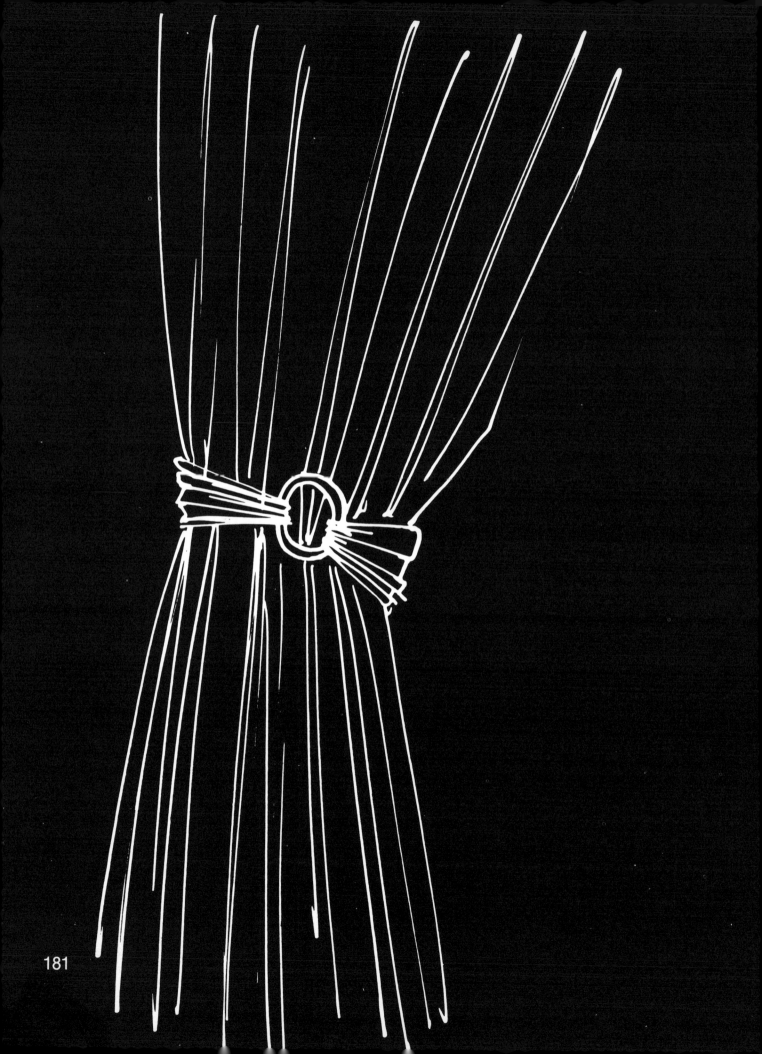

181

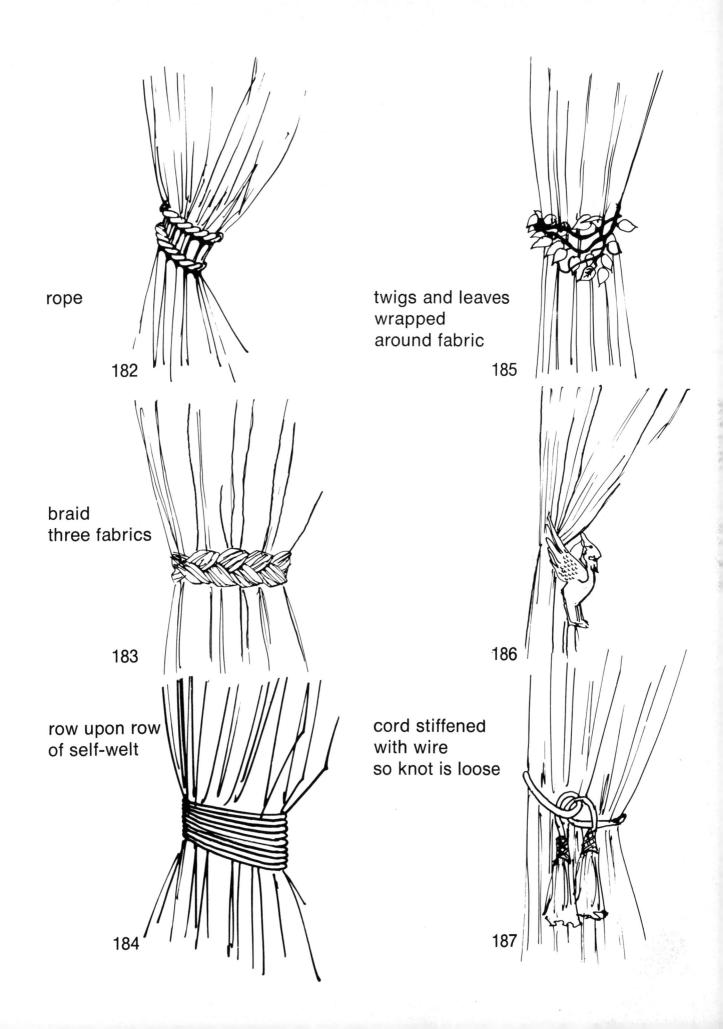

rope

182

braid
three fabrics

183

row upon row
of self-welt

184

twigs and leaves
wrapped
around fabric

185

186

cord stiffened
with wire
so knot is loose

187

wooden, plastic
or metal chains

obi

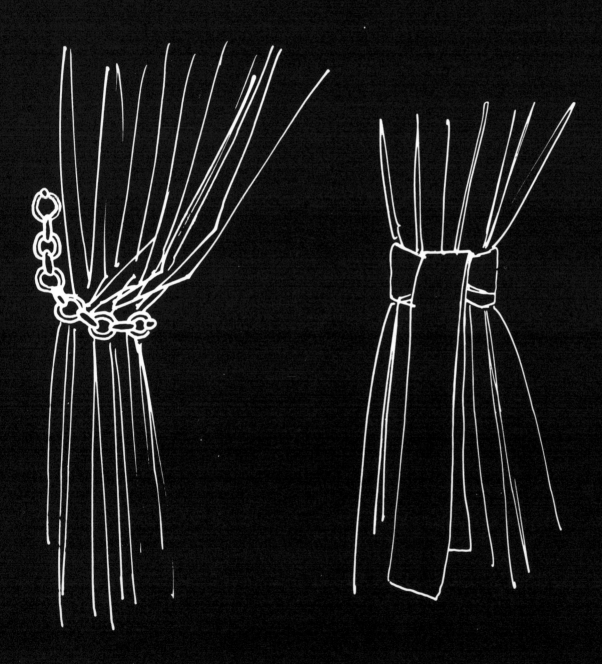

patent leather strap

crystal, ceramic, plastic
or metal strands of beads

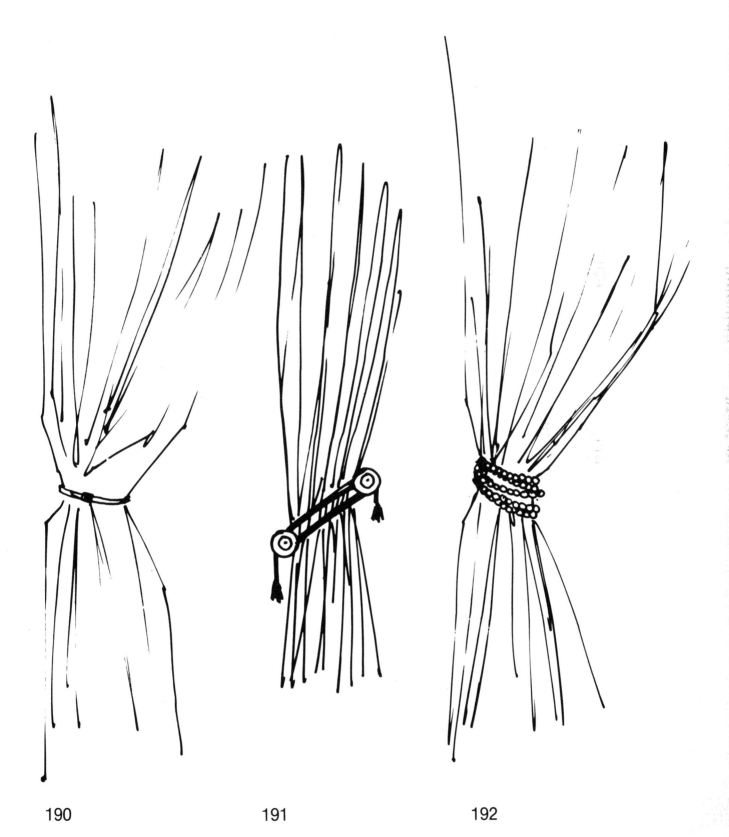

190   191   192

tape measure for sewing room   rag doll   for the nursery

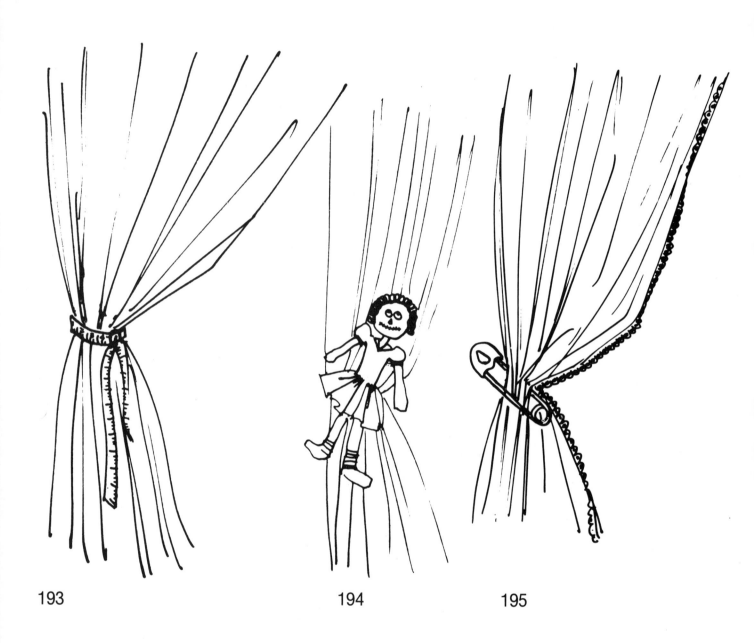

193   194   195

six-shooter   bandana   saddle leather

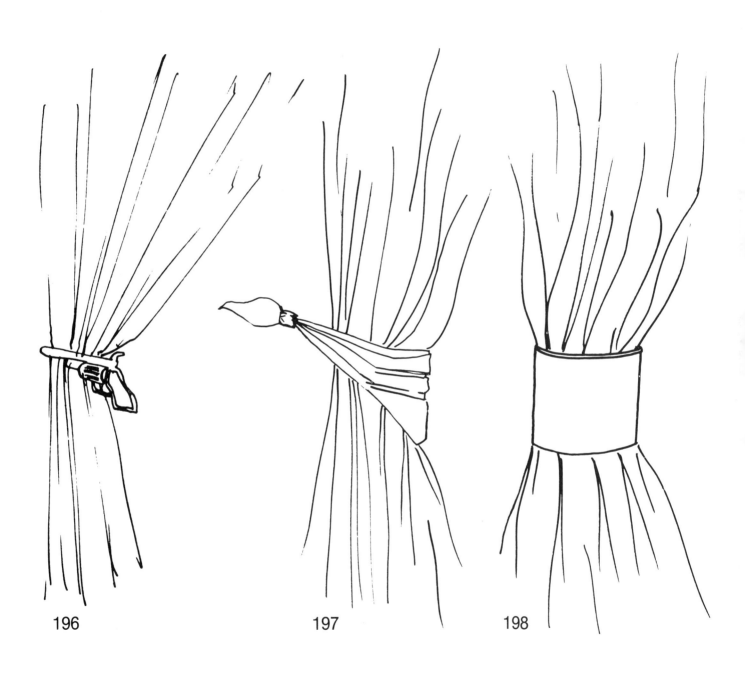

196   197   198

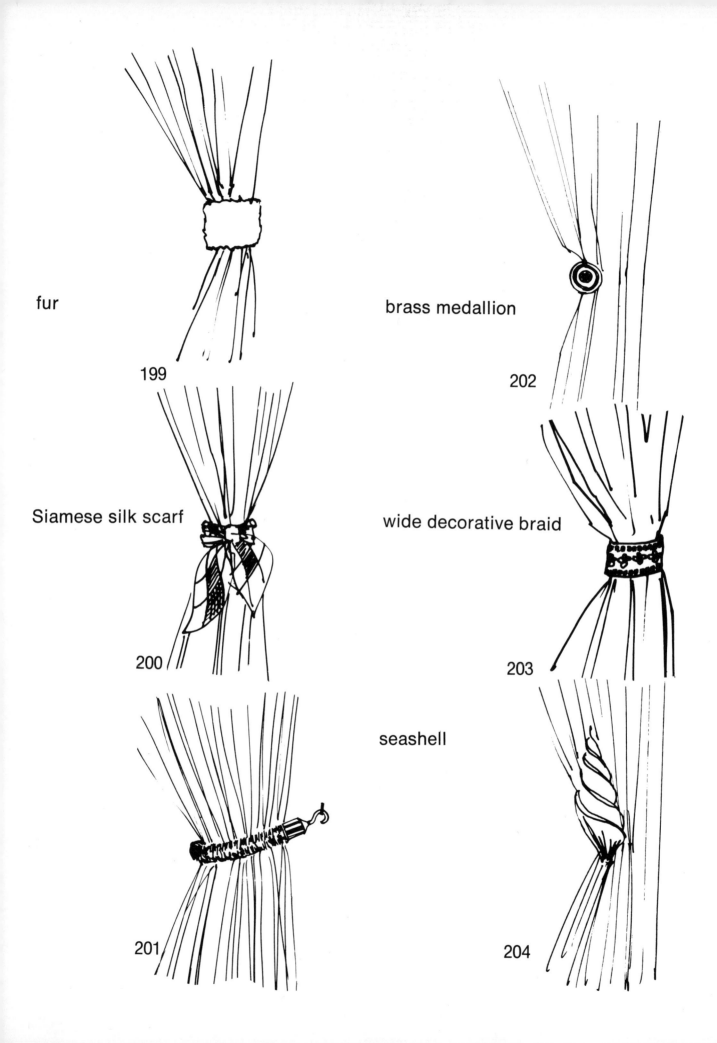

fur

199

brass medallion

202

Siamese silk scarf

200

wide decorative braid

203

seashell

201

204

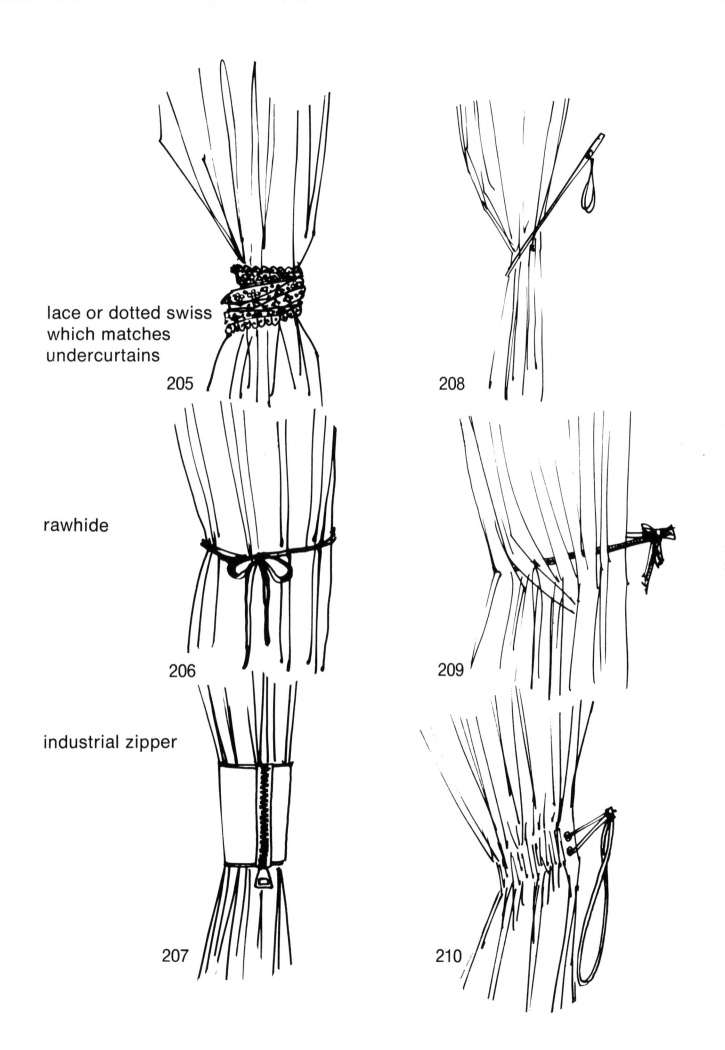

lace or dotted swiss
which matches
undercurtains

205

208

rawhide

206

209

industrial zipper

207

210

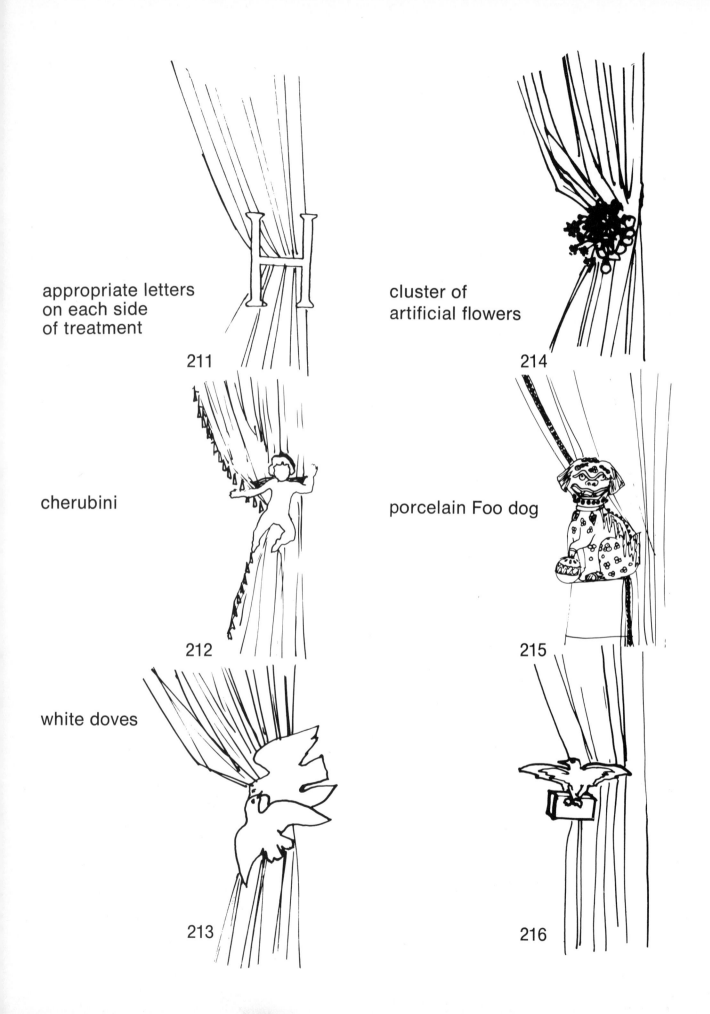

appropriate letters
on each side
of treatment

211

cherubini

212

white doves

213

cluster of
artificial flowers

214

porcelain Foo dog

215

216

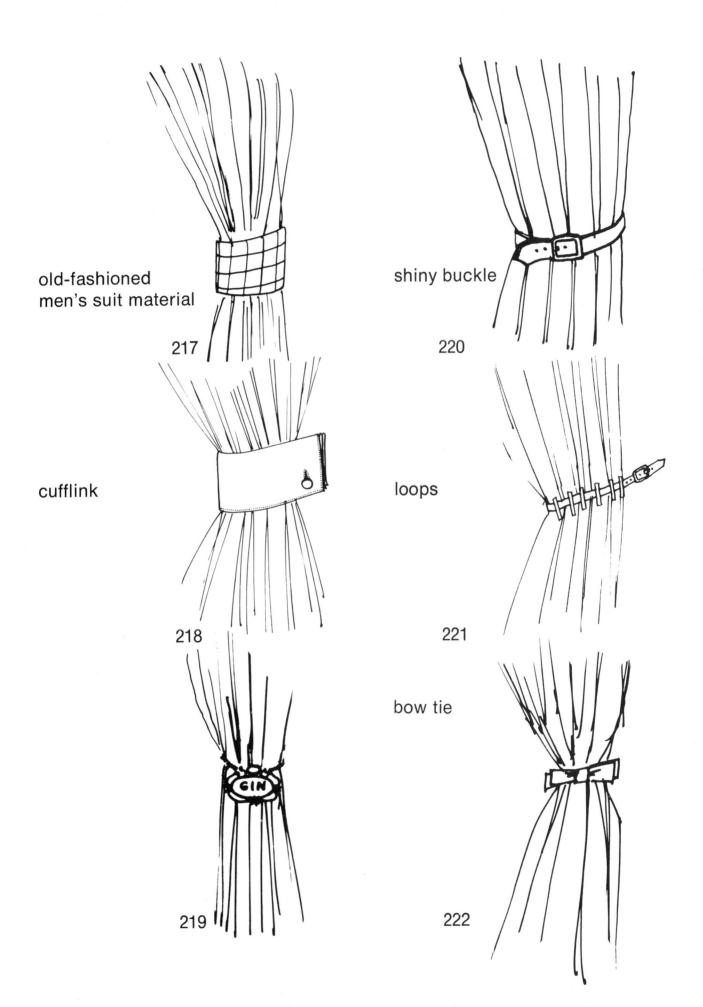

old-fashioned
men's suit material

217

cufflink

218

219

shiny buckle

220

loops

221

bow tie

222

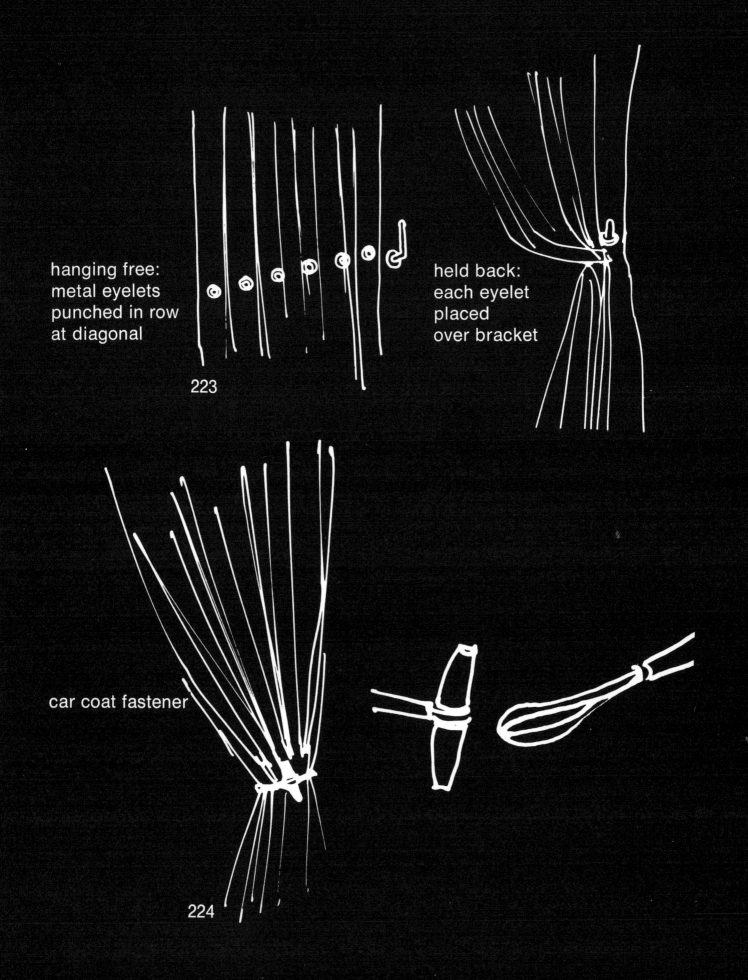

hanging free:
metal eyelets
punched in row
at diagonal

223

held back:
each eyelet
placed
over bracket

car coat fastener

224

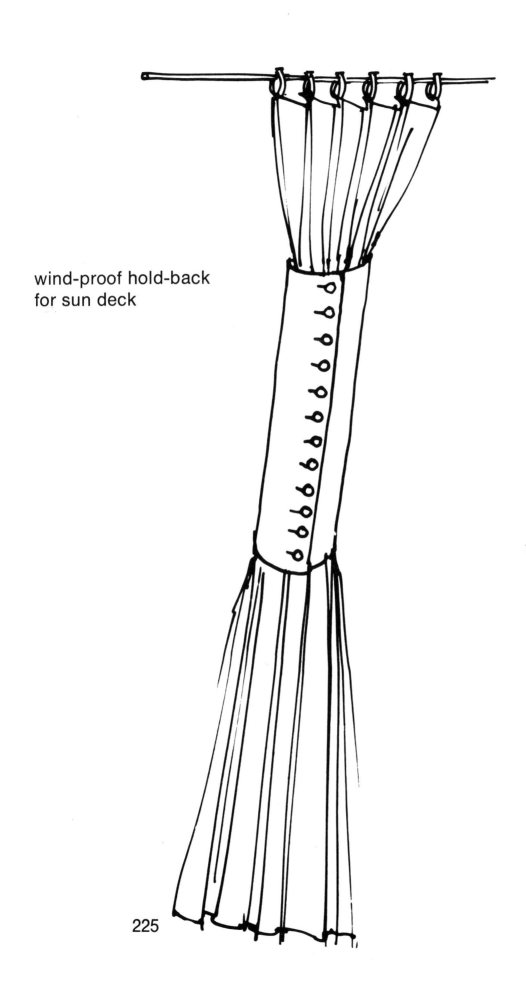

wind-proof hold-back
for sun deck

225

valances

226

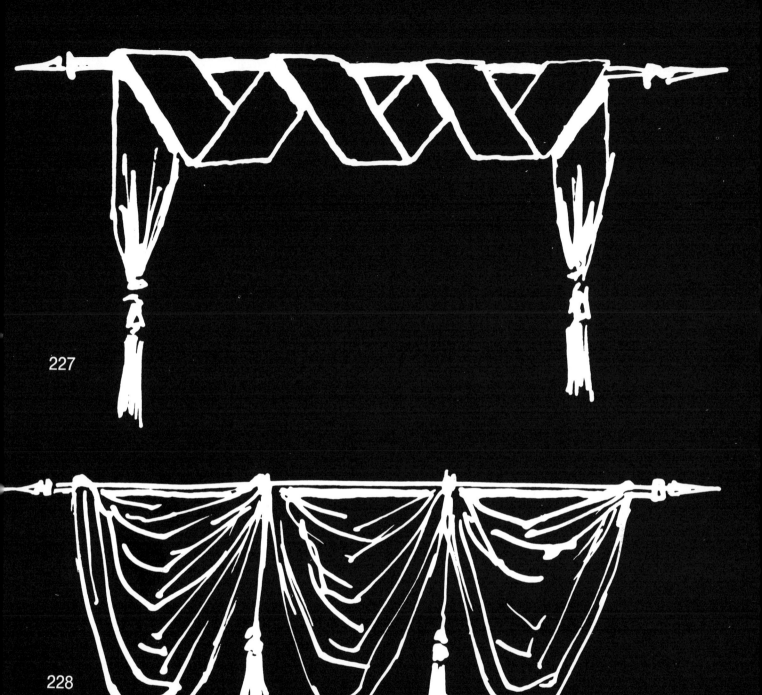

227

228

soft, straight
with alternate fabric
in pleats

229

two fabrics

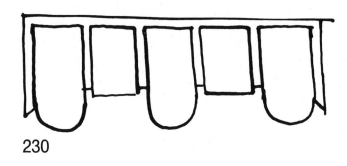

230

two fabrics

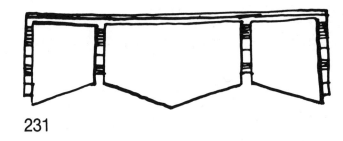

231

red, white, blue

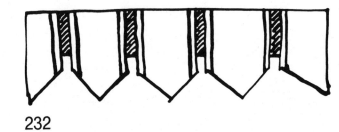

232

two poles with
separate pieces
of fabric

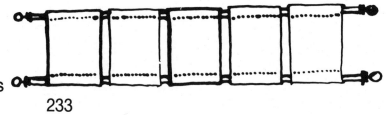

233

large red and black
farmer handkerchief
knotted at ends
for boy's room

234

swags over
shaped board

235

cord trim
soft swag bottom

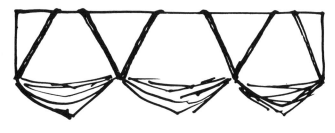

236

braid and buttons

237

second fabric
peeking through
draw-strings

238

239

240

241

fancy blazer buttons
with black fabric,
red fabric with
red covered button

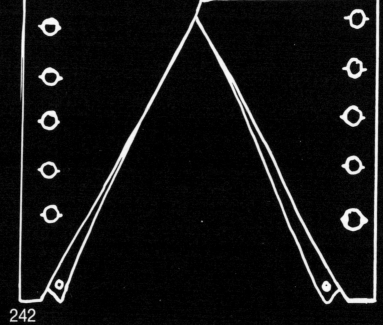

242

wide braid facing
on valance and bottom
of curtains

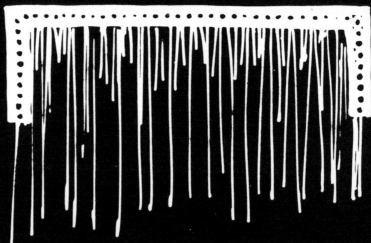

243

shirred fabric
in fan shape
wooden frame
cut out to form
floral pattern
and faced with
applied
decorative braid

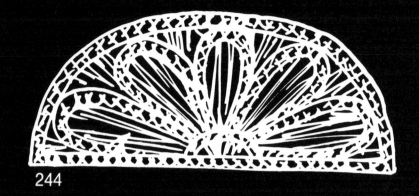

244

fabric thrown
over rod,
edges trimmed
with braid or fringe

245

bows made of
same braid
as edges of curtains

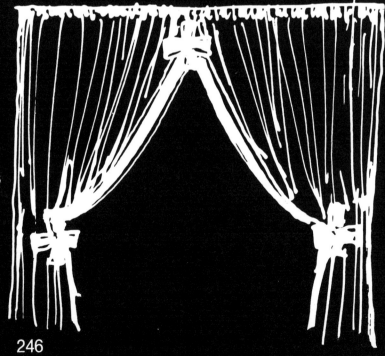

246

wooden frame faced
with decorative braid,
shirred fabric behind

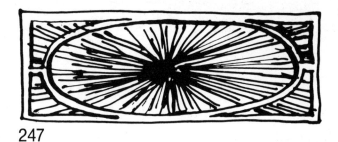

247

fabric shirred
over board
with painted wooden
moulding on top

248

braid trim with
shirred inserts

249

nailheads

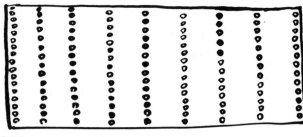

250

ribbon trim reversed
at each corner

251

design formed on
flat straight valance
by using
braid and tassels

252

same idea

253

poufy cotton tassels

254

tasseled lace fringe

255

print
plain fabric

256

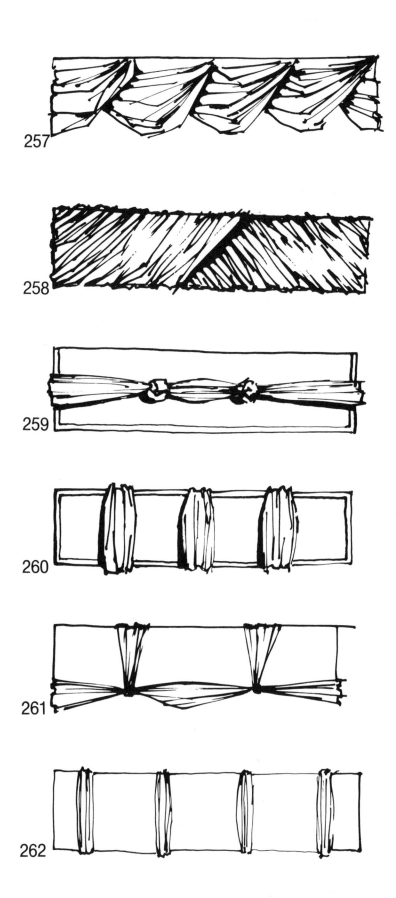

257

258

259

260

261

262

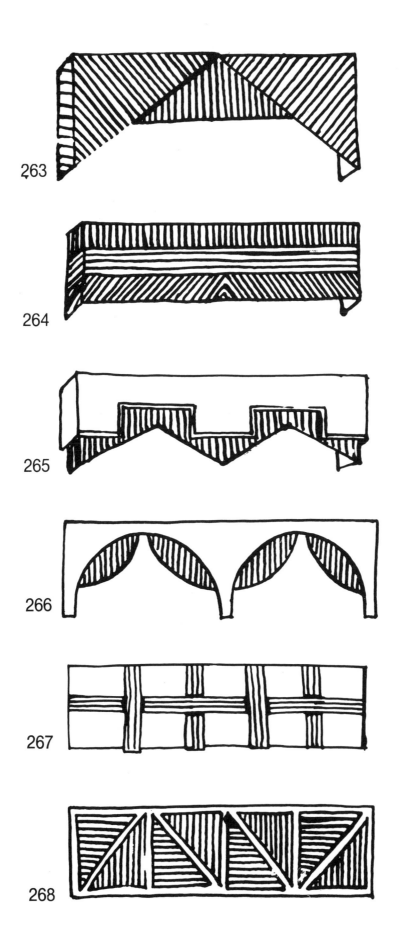

263

264

265

266

267

268

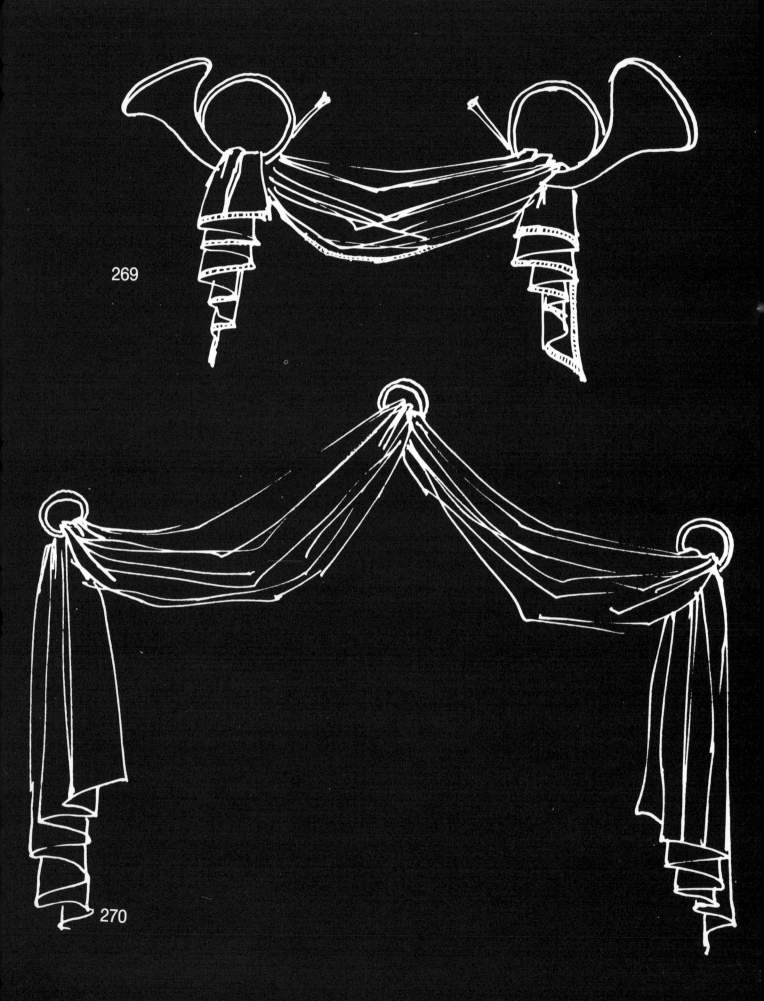

269

270

271

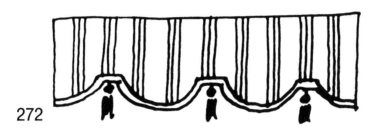

272

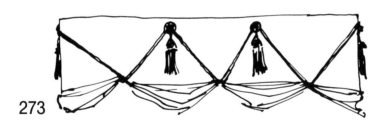

273

274

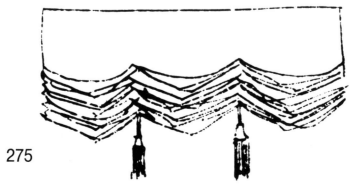

275

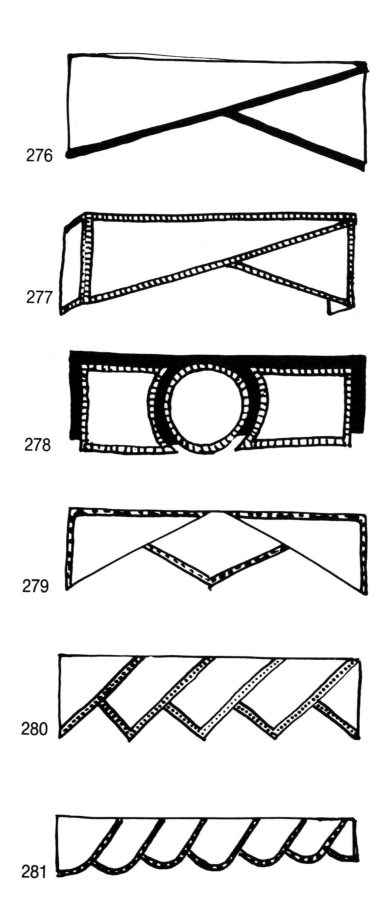

276

277

278

279

280

281

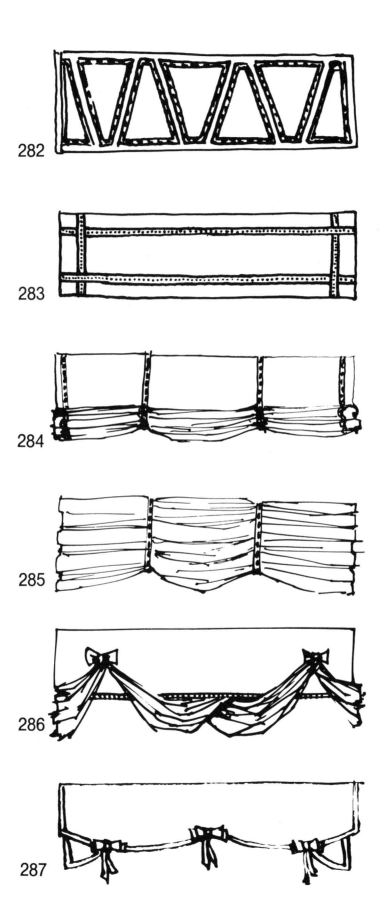

282

283

284

285

286

287

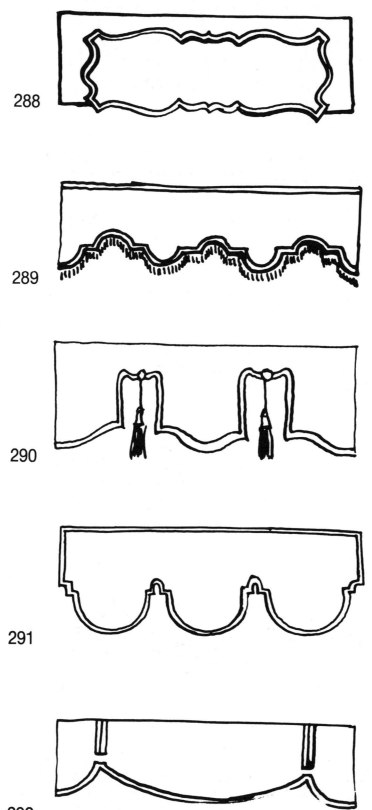

288

289

290

291

292

index

**period
designs**

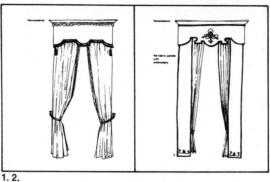

1. 2.

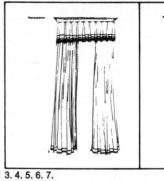

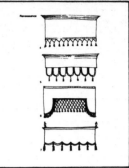

3. 4. 5. 6. 7.

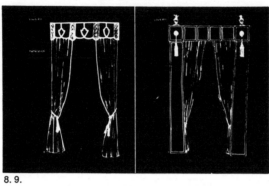

8. 9.

10. 11. 12. 13. 14.

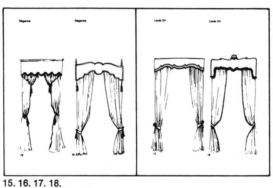

15. 16. 17. 18.

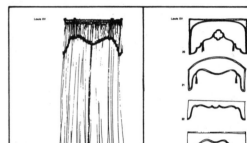

19. 20. 21. 22. 23.

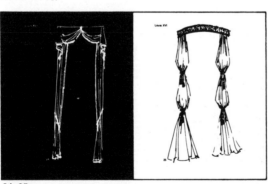

24. 25.

26. 27.

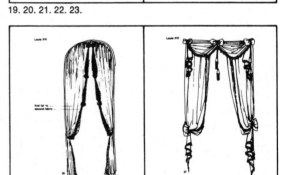

28. 29. 30. 31. 32. 33. 34. 35.

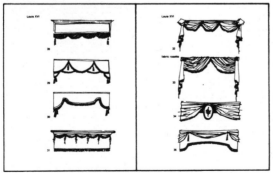

36. 37. 38. 39. 40. 41.

**period
designs**

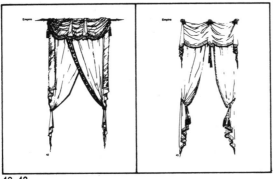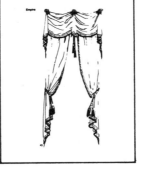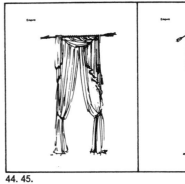

42. 43.

44. 45.

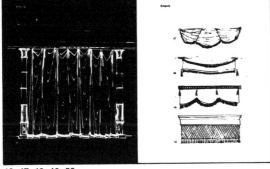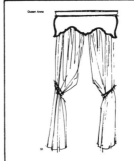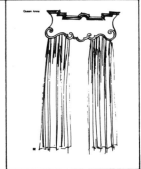

46. 47. 48. 49. 50.

51. 52.

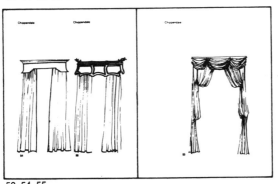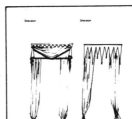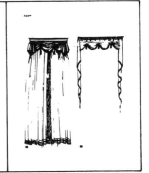

53. 54. 55.

56. 57. 58. 59.

60. 61.

**formal
designs**

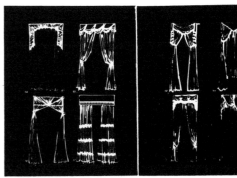

62. 63.

64. 65. 66. 67. 68. 69. 70. 71.

**formal
designs**

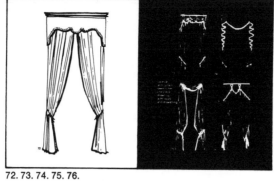
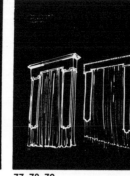
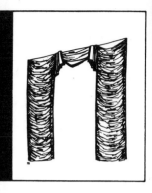

72. 73. 74. 75. 76.   77. 78. 79.

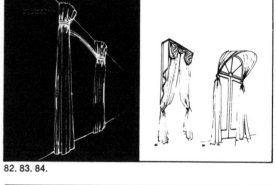

80. 81.   82. 83. 84.

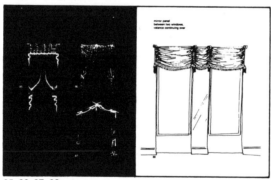
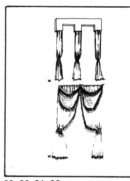
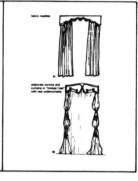

85. 86. 87. 88.   89. 90. 91. 92.

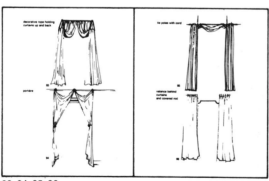
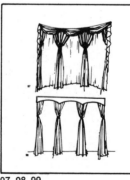
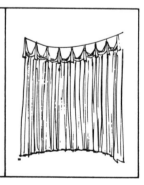

93. 94. 95. 96.   97. 98. 99.

100.   101. 102.

formal designs

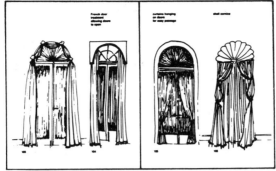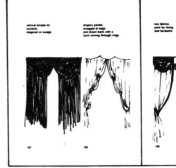

103. 104. 105. 106.   107. 108. 109. 110.

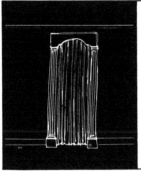   

111. 112.   113. 114.

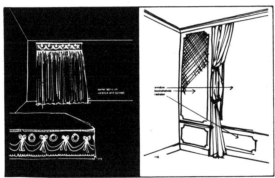

115. 116.

casual designs

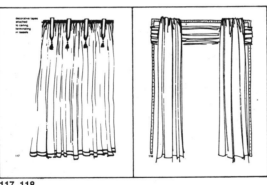

117. 118.   119. 120. 121.

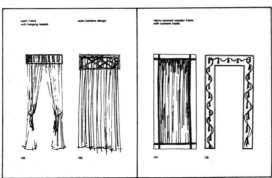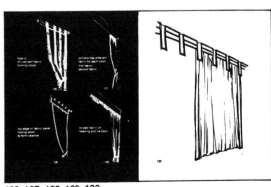

122. 123. 124. 125.   126. 127. 128. 129. 130.

**casual
designs**

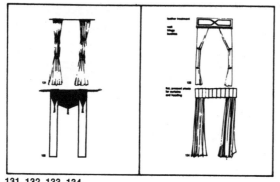

131. 132. 133. 134.

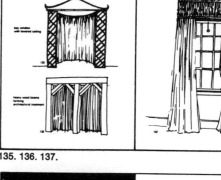

135. 136. 137.

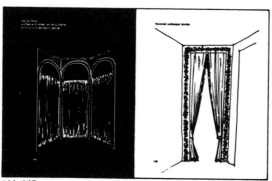

138. 139. 140. 141.

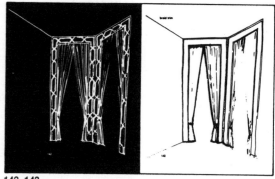

142. 143.

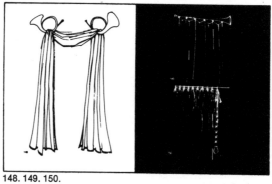

144. 145.

146. 147.

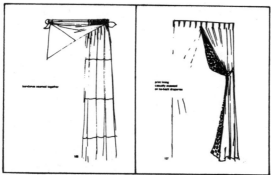

148. 149. 150.

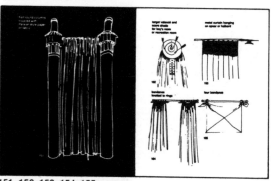

151. 152. 153. 154. 155.

156. 157.

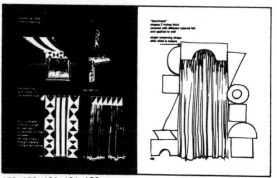

158. 159. 160. 161. 162.

casual designs

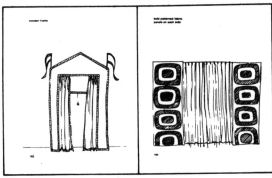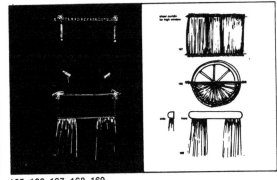

163. 164. 165. 166. 167. 168. 169.

headings

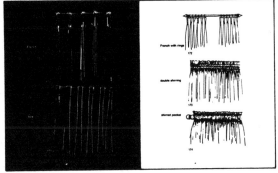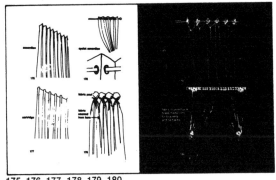

170. 171. 172. 173. 174. 175. 176. 177. 178. 179. 180.

tie-backs

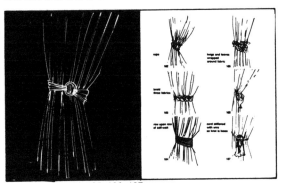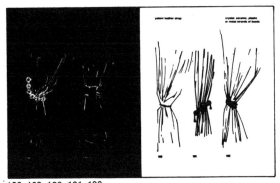

181. 182. 183. 184. 185. 186. 187. 188. 189. 190. 191. 192.

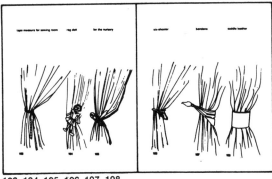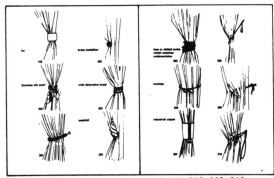

193. 194. 195. 196. 197. 198. 199. 200. 201. 202. 203. 204. 205. 206. 207. 208. 209. 210.

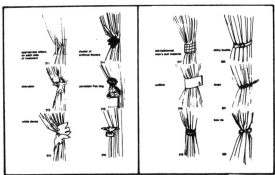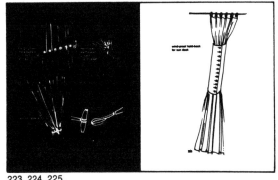

211. 212. 213. 214. 215. 216. 217. 218. 219. 220. 221. 222. 223. 224. 225.

valences

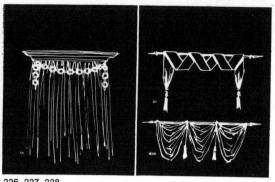
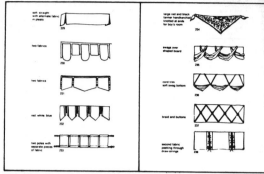

226. 227. 228.

229. 230. 231. 232. 233. 234. 235. 236. 237. 238.

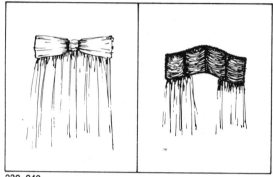
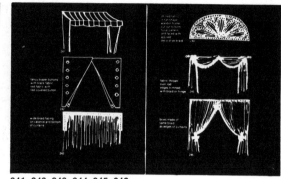

239. 240.

241. 242. 243. 244. 245. 246.

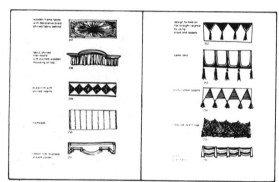
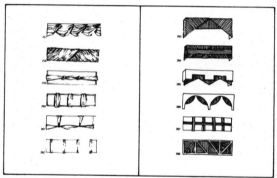

247. 248. 249. 250. 251. 252. 253. 254. 255. 256.

257. 258. 259. 260. 261. 262. 263. 264. 265. 266. 267. 268.

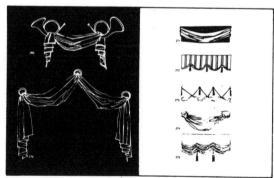
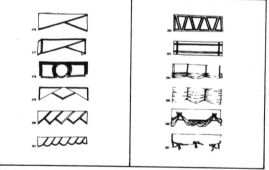

269. 270. 271. 272. 273. 274. 275.

276. 277. 278. 279. 280. 281. 282. 283. 284. 285. 286. 287.

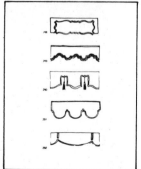

288. 289. 290. 291. 292.